OFFICIAL SQA PAST PAPERS WITH ANSWERS

STANDARD GRADE | GENERAL | CREDIT

ENGLISH
2008-2012

© Scottish Qualifications Authority
All rights reserved. Copying prohibited. No part of this publication may be reproduced, stored in a retrieval system, or transmitted in any form or by any means, electronic, mechanical, photocopying, recording or otherwise.

First exam published in 2008.
Published by Bright Red Publishing Ltd, 6 Stafford Street, Edinburgh EH3 7AU
tel: 0131 220 5804 fax: 0131 220 6710 info@brightredpublishing.co.uk www.brightredpublishing.co.uk

ISBN 978-1-84948-244-8

A CIP Catalogue record for this book is available from the British Library.

Bright Red Publishing is grateful to the copyright holders, as credited on the final page of the Question Section, for permission to use their material. Every effort has been made to trace the copyright holders and to obtain their permission for the use of copyright material.
Bright Red Publishing will be happy to receive information allowing us to rectify any error or omission in future editions.

STANDARD GRADE | GENERAL

2008
READING

[BLANK PAGE]

G

0860/403

NATIONAL
QUALIFICATIONS
2008

TUESDAY, 6 MAY
1.00 PM – 1.50 PM

ENGLISH
STANDARD GRADE
General Level
Reading
Text

Read carefully the passage overleaf. It will help if you read it twice. When you have done so, answer the questions. Use the spaces provided in the Question/Answer booklet.

Saddle the white horses

Thurso prepares to host its first professional surf tour, confirming Scotland's status as a world–class surfing destination.

1   It was the stickers that gave it away. Turning left on the A9 at Latheron in Caithness, you were suddenly faced with a sign that looked as though it had been defaced by advertising executives from surfing companies. Like a cairn on a mountain path, the big green board declaring Thurso to be 23 miles away told travelling bands of surfers that they'd taken the right turn-off and were nearly at their destination. Slapping another sticker on the sign was like laying another stone on the pile.

2   Thurso is about to enter surfing's big league.

3   It's hard to reconcile the popular tropical imagery of surfing with the town, a raw, exposed kind of place that enjoys little escape from the worst excesses of the Scottish climate. The Caithness coastline is peppered with surfing spots, but the jewel in the crown and the target for dedicated wave riders lies within spitting distance of Thurso town centre at a reef break called Thurso East. In the right conditions, the swell there rears up over kelp-covered slabs into a fast-moving, barrelling monster of a wave considered world class by those in the know.

4   Now Thurso East is the focus of a huge professional surfing tour. The week-long Highland Open marks the first time a World Qualifying Series (WQS) surfing competition has been held in Scotland. It will also be the furthest north a WQS tour has ever travelled, anywhere in the world.

5   Professional competitive surfing has two tours: the WQS and the World Championship Tour (WCT). The WCT is the premier division, with the WQS being used as a platform for professionals to move up into the big time. Around 160 up-and-coming wave riders are expected to take part in the Thurso event. Prize money of $100,000 (£57,000) is up for grabs, along with vital tour points.

6   "Travelling and exploring new places is part of the whole surfing culture," says Bernhard Ritzer, the Highland Open event manager. "We've had so much feedback from surfers from Australia and Brazil who want to go. They see it as an adventure and as something new. We did a photo trip there last year with some of our team riders and they were impressed. They're excited about it—although it will still be a shock because I don't think they know how cold and harsh it can be."

7   "Thurso is one of the best waves in Europe, if not the world," he says. "Most people don't even know it, and it's just so good. It doesn't always have to be sunny, warm and tropical. It can also be cold, rough and hard.

8   "The idea is to have a contrast to the summer events in the tropical islands. We also have something in the north to show that this is part of surfing. Very often on the WQS tour the waves aren't that good, but here they are expecting big reef break waves and they like to surf those."

9   Surfers generally guard their local breaks jealously. It's considered essential to keep your mouth shut about your "secret spot", in case you find it overrun with visitors. So, economic benefits to Thurso aside, some local surfers were a little concerned about an event on this scale descending on their area. WQS representatives met with these surfers to address their concerns and feel that they've pretty much got everyone on board. WQS is also paying for improvements to the car parking area near the Thurso East break.

10   "We're concerned to get the locals involved," says Ritzer. "We want to keep them happy and don't want to look too commercial, coming in with a big event machine. We need them to help organise local stuff. You always have some individuals who will boycott everything, but we understand that most of them are positive."

11   Andy Bain probably knows the break at Thurso East better than anyone, although he'll be watching the competition from the shoreline. Bain, who runs Thurso Surf, has been surfing the reef there for 17 years and is eagerly anticipating the arrival of the Highland Open. He's aware of the concerns and the possible exposure of his home break, but doesn't anticipate a negative impact.

12   "From the surf school side of things it's good because it'll generate business for us," says Bain, 33. "As a local surfer, it's kind of like closure for me to have this competition. To say the world has now recognised Thurso as a top surfing destination makes me feel proud. A lot of people say it's going to get crowded and exposed, but with it being a cold destination I don't think it's going to be that bad."

13   For professional surfer Adam Robertson from Victoria, Australia, the trip to Thurso will be something of a journey into the unknown. "This will be the first time I've ever been to Scotland," says Robertson, who has competed on the WQS tour for the past three years. "We're all a bit worried about how cold it's going to be. Apart from that we're pretty excited because it's a place we've never been."

14   Robertson, 23, who has been surfing since he was four, criss-crosses the globe with his fellow WQS competitors in pursuit of the best waves and a place on the coveted WCT tour. He may as well be going to surf on the moon for all he knows about Thurso East, but that's part of the appeal.

15   "We follow the surf around all year and go to a lot of different places, but Scotland's somewhere probably none of us have been to," he says. "That for me was a big part of wanting to go, to see the place. As a professional surfer, you've got to live out of your bag a lot, travelling around with long stints away from home, but when you perform well in the event or get some really good waves, it makes it all worth it.

16   "I feel pretty good and I'm hoping to do well," he adds. "Everyone who does the tour is feeling good too, so it should be a great event. It'll be interesting to see what the waves are like."

17   Competitors will be scored by a team of eight international judges on the length of their ride, the difficulty of moves and how they connect it all together. Waves are scored on a one to ten scale, with ten a perfect ride, and the final scores are based on each surfer's two highest-scoring waves.

18   "These events raise the profile of locations, create investment in areas and hopefully provide opportunities for young surfers coming through to grow and compete at world-class levels," says Dave Reed, contest director for the WQS event. "It's a great way to say we've got some of the best waves in the world."

Adapted from a magazine article

[END OF PASSAGE]

[BLANK PAGE]

FOR OFFICIAL USE

G

Total
Mark

0860/404

NATIONAL
QUALIFICATIONS
2008

TUESDAY, 6 MAY
1.00 PM – 1.50 PM

ENGLISH
STANDARD GRADE
General Level
Reading
Questions

Fill in these boxes and read what is printed below.

Full name of centre

Town

Forename(s)

Surname

Date of birth
Day   Month   Year

Scottish candidate number

Number of seat

NB Before leaving the examination room you must give this booklet to the invigilator. If you do not, you may lose all the marks for this paper.

SA 0860/404 6/66870

Marks

QUESTIONS

Write your answers in the spaces provided.

Look at Paragraphs 1 to 3.

1. (*a*)   What had been added to the road sign in Caithness?

   _____   2 ■ 0

   (*b*)   Write down **two** things the surfers would know when they saw this road sign.

   _____

   _____   2 1 0

2. "Thurso is about to enter surfing's big league." (Paragraph 2)

    How does the writer make this statement stand out?

    _____   2 ■ 0

3. Thurso is different from the popular image of a surfing location.

    (*a*)   **In your own words**, describe the popular image of a surfing location.

    _____   2 ■ 0

    (*b*)   **Write down an expression** showing how Thurso is different.

    _____   2 ■ 0

4. What do the words "jewel in the crown" (Paragraph 3) suggest about Thurso East?

    _____   2 ■ 0

5. ". . . a fast-moving, barrelling monster . . ." (Paragraph 3)

    Explain fully why this is an effective description of the wave.

    _____

    _____   2 1 0

PAGE
TOTAL

Marks

Look at Paragraphs 4 and 5.

6. In which **two** ways is the Highland Open different from other WQS surfing competitions?

   (i) _____

   (ii) _____   2 1 0

7. **In your own words**, explain the difference between the two professional surfing tours.

   WCT _____

   WQS _____   2 1 0

8. Which **two** benefits will the winner of the competition gain?

   (i) _____

   (ii) _____   2 1 0

Look at Paragraphs 6 to 8.

9. Give **three** reasons why, according to Bernhard Ritzer, surfers will want to visit Thurso.

   (i) _____

   (ii) _____

   (iii) _____   2 1 0

10. According to Ritzer, what will surprise the surfers?

    _____   2 ■ 0

[Turn over

Marks

11. Thurso can offer something which many other surfing locations cannot.

What is this?

_____   2 ■ 0

Look at Paragraphs 9 and 10.

12. "Surfers generally guard their local breaks . . . " (Paragraph 9)

In your own words, explain why surfers do this.

_____   2 1 0

13. What **style** of language is used in the expression "keep your mouth shut" (Paragraph 9)?

_____   2 ■ 0

14. Which **two key** things have WQS representatives done to gain support?

(i) _____

(ii) _____   2 1 0

15. The WQS representatives feel that "they've pretty much got everyone on board." (Paragraph 9)

Write down an expression from Paragraph 10 which continues this idea.

_____   2 ■ 0

16. Write down a single word from this section meaning "refuse to support or take part".

2 ■ 0

PAGE
TOTAL

Marks

Look at Paragraphs 11 to 18.

17. (*a*) How does local surfer Andy Bain feel about the competition?

Tick (✓) the best answer.

very negative and angry	
quite pleased but worried	
excited and not really anxious	

2 ■ 0

(*b*) **Write down an expression** to support your chosen answer.

_____

2 ■ 0

18. "He may as well be going to surf on the moon . . . " (Paragraph 14)

What does this comparison suggest about Thurso?

_____

2 ■ 0

19. In Paragraph 15, Australian Adam Robertson describes his life as a professional surfer.

In your own words, sum up the **negative** and **positive** aspects of his life.

(*a*) **negative:** _____

_____

2 1 0

(*b*) **positive:** _____

_____

2 1 0

20. What **three** elements of the surfers' performance are judged?

(i) _____

(ii) _____

(iii) _____

2 1 0

[Turn over

PAGE
TOTAL

Think about the passage as a whole.

21.   (i)   What do you think is the main purpose of this passage?

Tick (✓) **one** box.

to tell the reader some amusing stories about surfing	
to inform the reader about a surfing competition in Scotland	
to argue against holding a surfing competition in Scotland	

(ii)   Give a reason to support your answer.

_____

_____   2   1   0

[END OF QUESTION PAPER]

PAGE
TOTAL

FOR OFFICIAL USE

p2	
p3	
p4	
p5	
p6	
TOTAL MARK	

FOR OFFICIAL USE

[BLANK PAGE]

STANDARD GRADE | CREDIT

2008
READING

[BLANK PAGE]

C

0860/405

NATIONAL
QUALIFICATIONS
2008

TUESDAY, 6 MAY
2.30 PM – 3.20 PM

ENGLISH
STANDARD GRADE
Credit Level
Reading
Text

Read carefully the passage overleaf. It will help if you read it twice. When you have done so, answer the questions. Use the spaces provided in the Question/Answer booklet.

This passage, taken from the opening chapter of a novel, introduces us to the character of Briony and her family.

1   The play—for which Briony had designed the posters, programmes and tickets, constructed the sales booth out of a folding screen tipped on its side, and lined the collection box in red crêpe paper—was written by her in a two-day tempest of composition, causing her to miss a breakfast and a lunch. When the preparations were complete, she had nothing to do but contemplate her finished draft and wait for the appearance of her cousins from the distant north. There would be time for only one day of rehearsal before her brother, Leon, arrived.

2   At some moments chilling, at others desperately sad, the play told a tale of the heart whose message, conveyed in a rhyming prologue, was that love which did not build a foundation on good sense was doomed. The reckless passion of the heroine, Arabella, for a wicked foreign count is punished by ill fortune when she contracts cholera during an impetuous dash towards a seaside town with her intended. Deserted by him and nearly everybody else, bed-bound in an attic, she discovers in herself a sense of humour. Fortune presents her a second chance in the form of an impoverished doctor—in fact, a prince in disguise who has elected to work among the needy. Healed by him, Arabella chooses wisely this time, and is rewarded by reconciliation with her family and a wedding with the medical prince on "a windy sunlit day in spring".

3   Mrs Tallis read the seven pages of *The Trials of Arabella* in her bedroom, at her dressing table, with the author's arm around her shoulder the whole while. Briony studied her mother's face for every trace of shifting emotion, and Emily Tallis obliged with looks of alarm, snickers of glee and, at the end, grateful smiles and wise, affirming nods. She took her daughter in her arms, onto her lap, and said that the play was "stupendous", and agreed instantly, murmuring into the girl's ear, that this word could be quoted on the poster which was to be on an easel in the entrance hall by the ticket booth.

4   Briony was hardly to know it then, but this was the project's highest point of fulfilment. Nothing came near it for satisfaction, all else was dreams and frustration. There were moments in the summer dusk after her light was out, burrowing in the delicious gloom of her canopy bed, when she made her heart thud with luminous, yearning fantasies, little playlets in themselves, every one of which featured Leon. In one, his big, good-natured face buckled in grief as Arabella sank in loneliness and despair. In another, there he was, cocktail in hand at some fashionable city bar, overheard boasting to a group of friends: Yes, my younger sister, Briony Tallis the writer, you must surely have heard of her. In a third he punched the air in exultation as the final curtain fell, although there was no curtain, there was no possibility of a curtain. Her play was not for her cousins, it was for her brother, to celebrate his return, provoke his admiration and guide him away from his careless succession of girlfriends, towards the right form of wife, the one who would persuade him to return to the countryside, the one who would sweetly request Briony's services as a bridesmaid.

5   She was one of those children possessed by a desire to have the world just so. Whereas her big sister's room was a stew of unclosed books, unfolded clothes, unmade bed, unemptied ashtrays, Briony's was a shrine to her controlling demon: the model farm spread across a deep window ledge consisted of the usual animals, but all facing one way—towards their owner—as if about to break into song, and even the farmyard hens were neatly corralled. In fact, Briony's was the only tidy upstairs

room in the house. Her straight-backed dolls in their many-roomed mansion appeared to be under strict instructions not to touch the walls; the various thumb-sized figures to be found standing about her dressing table—cowboys, deep-sea divers, humanoid mice—suggested by their even ranks and spacing a citizen army awaiting orders.

6   A taste for the miniature was one aspect of an orderly spirit. Another was a passion for secrets: in a prized varnished cabinet, a secret drawer was opened by pushing against the grain of a cleverly turned dovetail joint, and here she kept a diary locked by a clasp, and a notebook written in a code of her own invention. In a toy safe opened by six secret numbers she stored letters and postcards. An old tin petty cash box was hidden under a removable floorboard beneath her bed. In the box were treasures that dated back four years, to her ninth birthday when she began collecting: a mutant double acorn, fool's gold, a rain-making spell bought at a funfair, a squirrel's skull as light as a leaf.

7   At the age of eleven she wrote her first story—a foolish affair, imitative of half a dozen folk tales and lacking, she realised later, that vital knowingness about the ways of the world which compels a reader's respect. But this first clumsy attempt showed her that the imagination itself was a source of secrets: once she had begun a story, no one could be told. Pretending in words was too tentative, too vulnerable, too embarrassing to let anyone know. Even writing out the *she says*, the *and thens*, made her wince, and she felt foolish, appearing to know about the emotions of an imaginary being. Self-exposure was inevitable the moment she described a character's weakness; the reader was bound to speculate that she was describing herself. What other authority could she have? Only when a story was finished could she feel immune, and ready to punch holes in the margins, bind the chapters with pieces of string, paint or draw the cover, and take the finished work to show to her mother, or her father, when he was home.

8   Her efforts received encouragement. In fact, they were welcomed as the Tallises began to understand that the baby of the family possessed a strange mind and a facility with words. Briony was encouraged to read her stories aloud in the library and it surprised her parents and older sister to hear their quiet girl perform so boldly, making big gestures with her free arm, arching her eyebrows as she did the voices, and looking up from the page for seconds at a time as she read in order to gaze into one face after the other, unapologetically demanding her family's total attention as she cast her narrative spell.

9   The play she had written for Leon's homecoming was her first attempt at drama, and she had found the change quite effortless. It was a relief not to be writing out the *she says*, or describing the weather or the onset of spring or her heroine's face—beauty, she had discovered, occupied a narrow band. Ugliness, on the other hand, had infinite variation. *The Trials of Arabella* was intended to inspire not laughter, but terror, relief and instruction, in that order, and the innocent intensity with which Briony set about the project—the posters, tickets, sales booth—made her particularly vulnerable to failure.

[END OF PASSAGE]

[BLANK PAGE]

FOR OFFICIAL USE

C

Total Mark

0860/406

NATIONAL
QUALIFICATIONS
2008

TUESDAY, 6 MAY
2.30 PM – 3.20 PM

ENGLISH
STANDARD GRADE
Credit Level
Reading
Questions

Fill in these boxes and read what is printed below.

Full name of centre

Town

Forename(s)

Surname

Date of birth
Day Month Year   Scottish candidate number   Number of seat

**NB Before leaving the examination room you must give this booklet to the invigilator.
If you do not, you may lose all the marks for this paper.**

Marks

QUESTIONS

Write your answers in the spaces provided.

Look at Paragraph 1.

1. What task has Briony been involved in?

_____   2 ■ 0

2. In Paragraph 1, the writer shows how committed Briony has been to this task.

Explain how **sentence structure** and **word choice** indicate Briony's high level of commitment.

   (*a*)   **sentence structure:**

   _____

   _____   2 1 0

   (*b*)   **word choice:**

   _____

   _____   2 1 0

Look at Paragraph 2.

3. Briony's play is a story with a message.

In your own words, explain what the message is.

_____

_____   2 1 0

PAGE
TOTAL

Marks

4. Read the writer's description of Briony's play in Paragraph 2, beginning: "The reckless passion of the heroine . . ."

   (*a*) What seems to be the writer's attitude to Briony's play?

   _____   **2 1 0**

   (*b*) Quote **one** detail from the description and explain how it conveys this attitude.

   _____

   _____

   _____   **2 1 0**

Look at Paragraph 3.

5. ". . . and Emily Tallis obliged . . ." (Paragraph 3)

   What does the word "**obliged**" suggest about Emily's reaction to the play?

   _____   **2 ■ 0**

6. Give **two** ways in which the writer emphasises the closeness between Briony and her mother.

   (i) _____

   (ii) _____   **2 1 0**

Look at Paragraphs 4 and 5.

7. We are told that Briony's imagination took over "after her light was out". (Paragraph 4)

   By **referring closely** to the passage, **explain** how the writer's word choice indicates the **intensity** of Briony's fantasies.

   _____

   _____   **2 1 0**

[Turn over

PAGE
TOTAL

Marks

8. How does Briony want her brother, Leon, to **feel** about her writing?

Quote an expression from the passage to support your answer.

_____

_____   2 1 0

9. Look closely at the **final sentence** of Paragraph 4.

In your own words, give **two** reasons why Briony has written the play for her brother.

_____

_____   2 1 0

10. In Paragraph 5, the writer develops a **contrast** between Briony and her big sister.

(*a*) **In your own words**, state what the contrast is.

_____

_____   2 1 0

(*b*) By referring to **sentence structure** and **word choice**, explain how this contrast is developed.

You should refer to **both** characters in **both** parts of your answer.

(i) **sentence structure:** _____

_____

_____

_____   2 1 0

(ii) **word choice:** _____

_____

_____

_____   2 1 0

Marks

11. Explain the function of the **dashes** in the expression "— towards their owner—". (Paragraph 5)

_____ | 2 | 1 | 0

Look at Paragraph 6.

12. "Another was a passion for secrets:" (Paragraph 6)

    By referring to the passage, show how the writer continues this idea in the rest of the paragraph.

    _____

    _____ | 2 | 1 | 0

13. Explain why a **colon** is used in the expression "when she began collecting:" (Paragraph 6)

    _____ | 2 | 1 | 0

14. What do the items in Briony's collection suggest about her as a person?

    _____ | 2 | ■ | 0

Look at Paragraph 7.

15. Briony wrote her first story when she was eleven.

    In your own words, give **two** reasons why she later disliked this story.

    (i) _____

    (ii) _____ | 2 | 1 | 0

16. Explain **in your own words** why Briony was concerned about describing a character's weakness.

    _____

    _____ | 2 | 1 | 0

[Turn over for Questions 17 to 20 on *Page six*

PAGE TOTAL

Marks

17. **Quote one** word from Paragraph 7 showing that Briony was no longer vulnerable when the story was finished.

2 ■ 0

Look at Paragraphs 8 and 9.

18. Explain why Briony's performance in the library surprised her family.

Answer in your own words.

_____

_____

2 1 0

19. Why did Briony prefer writing about **ugly** rather than **beautiful** characters?

Use your own words in your explanation.

_____

_____

2 1 0

Think about the passage as a whole.

20. In Briony, the writer has created a character who is both **imaginative** and **anxious**.

By referring closely to the passage, show how both these aspects of her personality have been conveyed to the reader.

(i) **imaginative:**

_____

_____

2 1 0

(ii) **anxious:**

_____

_____

2 1 0

[END OF QUESTION PAPER]

PAGE
TOTAL

[BLANK PAGE]

G

0860/403

NATIONAL
QUALIFICATIONS
2009

FRIDAY, 8 MAY
1.00 PM – 1.50 PM

ENGLISH
STANDARD GRADE
General Level
Reading
Text

Read carefully the passage overleaf. It will help if you read it twice. When you have done so,
answer the questions. Use the spaces provided in the Question/Answer booklet.

In the following passage, Alice, the main character, is spending the summer working in France.

1   Alice notices a fly on the underside of her arm.

2   Insects are an occupational hazard at a dig, and for some reason there are more flies higher up the mountain where she is working than at the main excavation site lower down.

3   Her concentration broken, Alice stands up and stretches. She unscrews the top of her water bottle. It's warm, but she's too thirsty to care and drinks it down in great gulps. Below, the heat haze shimmers above the dented tarmac of the road. Above her, the sky is an endless blue.

4   It's her first time in the Pyrenees, although she feels very much at home. In the main camp on the lower slopes, Alice can see her colleagues standing under the big canvas awning. She's surprised they've stopped already. It's early in the day to be taking a break, but then the whole team is a bit demoralised. It's hard work: the digging, scraping, cataloguing, recording, and so far they've turned up little to justify their efforts. They've come across only a few fragments of early medieval pots and bowls, and a couple of arrowheads.

5   Alice is tempted to go down and join her colleagues. Her calves are already aching from squatting. The muscles in her shoulders are tense. But she knows that if she stops now, she'll lose her momentum.

6   Hopefully, her luck's about to change. Earlier, she'd noticed something glinting beneath a large boulder, propped against the side of the mountain, almost as if it had been placed there by a giant hand. Although she can't make out what the object is, even how big it is, she's been digging all morning and she doesn't think it will be much longer before she can reach it.

7   She knows she should fetch someone. Alice is not a trained archaeologist, just a volunteer. But it's her last day on site and she wants to prove herself. If she goes back down to the main camp now and admits she's on to something, everybody will want to be involved, and it will no longer be her discovery.

8   In the days and weeks to come, Alice will look back to this moment. She will wonder at how different things might have been had she made the choice to go and not to stay. If she had played by the rules.

9   She drains the last drop of water from the bottle and tosses it into her rucksack. For the next hour or so, as the sun climbs higher in the sky and the temperature rises, Alice carries on working. The only sounds are the scrape of metal on rock, the whine of insects and the occasional buzz of a light aircraft in the distance.

10   Alice kneels down on the ground and leans her cheek and shoulder against the rock for support. Then, with a flutter of excitement, she pushes her fingers deep into the dark earth. Straight away, she knows she's got something worth finding. It is smooth to the touch, metal not stone. Grasping it firmly and telling herself not to expect too much, slowly, slowly she eases the object out into the light.

11   The rich, cloying smell of wet soil fills her nose and throat, although she barely notices. She is already lost in the past, captivated by the piece of history she cradles in the palms of her hands. It is a heavy, round buckle, speckled black and green with age and from its long burial.

12   Alice is so absorbed that she doesn't notice the boulder shifting on its base. Then something makes her look up. For a split second, the world seems to hang suspended, out of space, out of time. She is mesmerised by the ancient slab of stone as it sways and tilts, and then gracefully begins to fall towards her. At the very last moment, the light fractures. The spell is broken. Alice throws herself out of the way, half tumbling, half slithering sideways, just in time to avoid being crushed. The boulder hits the ground with a dull thud, sending up a cloud of pale brown dust, then rolls over and over, as if in slow motion, until it comes to rest further down the mountain.

13   Alice clutches desperately at the bushes and scrub to stop herself slipping any further. For a moment she lies sprawled in the dirt, dizzy and disorientated. As it sinks in how very close she came to being crushed, she turns cold. Takes a deep breath. Waits for the world to stop spinning.

14   Gradually, the pounding in her head dies away. The sickness in her stomach settles and everything starts to return to normal, enough for her to sit up and take stock. Her knees are grazed and streaked with blood and she's knocked her wrist where she landed awkwardly, still clutching the buckle in her hand to protect it, but basically she's escaped with no more than a few cuts and bruises.

15   She gets to her feet and dusts herself down. She raises her hand, is about to call out to attract someone's attention when she notices that there's a narrow opening visible in the side of the mountain where the boulder had been standing. Like a doorway cut into the rock.

16   She hesitates. Alice knows she should get somebody to come with her. It is stupid, possibly even dangerous, to go in on her own without any sort of back-up. She knows all the things that can go wrong. But something is drawing her in. It feels personal. It's her discovery.

17   She climbs back up. There is a dip in the ground at the mouth of the cave, where the stone had stood guard. The damp earth is alive with the frantic writhing of worms and beetles exposed suddenly to the light and heat after so long. Her cap lies on the ground where it fell. Her trowel is there too, just where she left it.

18   Alice peers into the darkness. The opening is no more than five feet high and about three feet wide and the edges are irregular and rough. It seems to be natural rather than man-made.

19   Slowly, her eyes become accustomed to the gloom. Velvet black gives way to charcoal grey and she sees that she is looking into a long, narrow tunnel.

20   Squeezing the buckle tightly in her hand, she takes a deep breath and steps forward into the passageway. Straight away, the smell of long-hidden, underground air surrounds her, filling her mouth and throat and lungs. It's cool and damp, not the dry, poisonous gases of a sealed cave she's been warned about, so she guesses there must be some source of fresh air.

21   Feeling nervous and slightly guilty, Alice wraps the buckle in a handkerchief and pushes it into her pocket, then cautiously steps forward.

22   As she moves further in, she feels the chill air curl around her bare legs and arms like a cat. She is walking downhill. She can feel the ground sloping away beneath her feet, uneven and gritty. The scrunch of the stones and gravel is loud in the confined, hushed space. She is aware of the daylight getting fainter and fainter at her back, the further and deeper she goes.

23   Abruptly, she does not want to go on.

Adapted from the novel "Labyrinth" by Kate Mosse

[END OF PASSAGE]

[BLANK PAGE]

FOR OFFICIAL USE

G

Total Mark

0860/404

NATIONAL
QUALIFICATIONS
2009

FRIDAY, 8 MAY
1.00 PM – 1.50 PM

ENGLISH
STANDARD GRADE
General Level
Reading
Questions

Fill in these boxes and read what is printed below.

Full name of centre

Town

Forename(s)

Surname

Date of birth
  Day Month Year

Scottish candidate number

Number of seat

NB Before leaving the examination room you must give this booklet to the invigilator. If you do not, you may lose all the marks for this paper.

SA 0860/404 6/63420

Marks

QUESTIONS

Write your answers in the spaces provided.

Look at Paragraphs 1 and 2.

1. What activity is Alice involved in?

    _____   2 ■ 0

2. "Insects are an occupational hazard . . . " (Paragraph 2)

    Explain **in your own words** what this means.

    _____

    _____   2 1 0

Look at Paragraphs 3 to 5.

3. Write down **three** things the writer tells us in Paragraph 3 which show that it is a hot day.

    (i) _____

    (ii) _____

    (iii) _____   2 1 0

4. How does the writer emphasise that "It's hard work"? (Paragraph 4)

    (*a*) by sentence structure

    _____   2 ■ 0

    (*b*) by word choice

    _____   2 ■ 0

5. Write down an expression from the passage which suggests the hard work has not been worth it so far.

    _____   2 ■ 0

PAGE
TOTAL

Marks

6. "Alice is tempted to go down and join her colleagues." (Paragraph 5)

Give **two** reasons why she is tempted to do this.

(i) _____

(ii) _____   2   1   0

Look at Paragraph 7.

7. Tick (✓) the appropriate box to show whether the following statements about Alice are True, False or Cannot Tell from the passage.

	True	False	Cannot Tell			
She wants to show that she can do the job herself.				2	■	0
She does not like her colleagues.				2	■	0
She wants to share her discovery.				2	■	0

Look at Paragraph 10.

8. In Paragraph 10, the writer shows Alice's **feelings** and **thoughts** as she pushes her hand into the soil.

(*a*) **Write down one** expression which shows her **feelings** at this point.

_____   2   ■   0

(*b*) **Write down one** expression which shows her **thoughts** at this point.

_____   2   ■   0

9. Why does the writer repeat the word "slowly" in Paragraph 10?

_____   2   ■   0

[Turn over

PAGE TOTAL

Marks

Look at Paragraphs 11 and 12.

10. Alice is "captivated" by the buckle she has found. (Paragraph 11)

    Write down **one** other word from the next paragraph (Paragraph 12) which **also** shows how interested she is in the buckle.

    2 ■ 0

11. Give **two** reasons why Alice does not move out of the way of the boulder until the last moment.

    (i) _____

    (ii) _____

    2 1 0

12. Explain carefully what is surprising about the word "gracefully" in Paragraph 12.

    _____

    2 1 0

Look at Paragraphs 13 to 16.

13. " . . . dirt, dizzy and disorientated." (Paragraph 13)

    Identify the **technique** used here.

    _____

    2 ■ 0

14. **In your own words**, explain why Alice "turns cold". (Paragraph 13)

    _____

    _____

    2 1 0

15. Why do you think Alice does **not** "call out to attract someone's attention"? (Paragraph 15)

    _____

    _____

    2 1 0

PAGE TOTAL

Marks

Look at Paragraphs 17 to 19.

16. ". . . the stone had stood guard." (Paragraph 17)

Give **two** reasons why this expression is appropriate.

(i) _____

(ii) _____   2   1   0

17. "Slowly, her eyes become accustomed to the gloom." (Paragraph 19)

Explain how the writer develops this idea in the next sentence.

_____

_____   2   1   0

Look at Paragraph 21 to the end of the passage.

18. As Alice steps into the tunnel, she experiences **two** feelings. **In your own words**, explain what these **two** feelings are.

(i) _____

(ii) _____   2   1   0

19. "Abruptly, she does not want to go on." (Paragraph 23)

Give **two** reasons why this is an effective ending to the passage.

(i) _____

(ii) _____   2   1   0

[Turn over

PAGE
TOTAL

Marks

Think about the passage as a whole.

20. The writer has written this story in the present tense.

    Why do you think the writer has done this?

    _____   2 ■ 0

21. What do you think will happen next in the story?

    Tick (✓) the answer which you think is most likely.

Alice will return to her colleagues.	
Alice will go further into the cave and make an exciting discovery.	
Alice will be trapped in the cave.	

    Give **two** pieces of evidence from the passage to support your answer.

    (i) _____

    (ii) _____   2 1 0

[END OF QUESTION PAPER]

PAGE
TOTAL

FOR OFFICIAL USE

[0860/404]

p2	
p3	
p4	
p5	
p6	
TOTAL MARK	

FOR OFFICIAL USE

[BLANK PAGE]

STANDARD GRADE | CREDIT

2009
READING

[BLANK PAGE]

C

0860/405

NATIONAL
QUALIFICATIONS
2009

FRIDAY, 8 MAY
2.30 PM – 3.20 PM

ENGLISH
STANDARD GRADE
Credit Level
Reading
Text

Read carefully the passage overleaf. It will help if you read it twice. When you have done so, answer the questions. Use the spaces provided in the Question/Answer booklet.

In the following passage, taken from a novel, the narrator, Christopher, has a frightening experience.

1   It was a sunny, windy morning. I remember watching from the playroom windows the leaves blowing in the front yard over the carriage track. Uncle Philip had been downstairs with my mother since shortly after breakfast, and I had been able to relax for a while, believing as I did that nothing could happen to her while he was with her.

2   Then midway through the morning I heard Uncle Philip calling me. I went out on to the landing and, looking down over the balcony rail, saw my mother and Uncle Philip standing in the hall, gazing up at me. For the first time in weeks I sensed something cheerful about them, as though they had just been enjoying a joke. The front door was ajar and a long streak of sunlight was falling across the hall. Uncle Philip said:

3   "Look here, Christopher. You're always saying you want a piano accordion. Well, I intend to buy you one. I spotted an excellent one in a window in Hankow Road yesterday. I propose the two of us go and look it over. If it takes your fancy, then it's yours. Good plan?"

4   This brought me down the staircase at great speed. I jumped the last four steps and circled round the adults, flapping my arms in impersonation of a bird of prey. As I did so, to my delight, I heard my mother laughing; laughing in a way I had not heard her laugh for a while. In fact it is possible it was this very atmosphere—this feeling that things were perhaps starting to return to what they had been—which played a significant part in causing me to "lower my guard". I asked Uncle Philip when we could go, to which he shrugged and said:

5   "Why not now? If we leave it, someone else might spot it. Perhaps someone's buying it at this moment, even as we speak!"

6   I rushed to the doorway and again my mother laughed. Then she told me I would have to put on proper shoes and a jacket. I remember thinking of protesting about the jacket, but then deciding not to in case the adults changed their minds, not only about the accordion, but also about this whole light-hearted mood we were enjoying.

7   I waved casually to my mother as Uncle Philip and I set off across the front courtyard. Then several steps on, as I was hurrying towards the waiting carriage, Uncle Philip grasped me by the shoulder, saying: "Look! Wave to your mother!" despite my already having done so. But I thought nothing of it at the time, and turning as bidden, waved once more to my mother's figure, elegantly upright in the doorway.

8   For much of the way, the carriage followed the route my mother and I usually took to the city centre. Uncle Philip was quiet, which surprised me a little, but I assumed this was perhaps his normal custom on a journey. Whenever I pointed out to him anything we were passing, he would reply cheerfully enough; but the next moment he would be staring silently once more out at the view. The leafy boulevards gave way to the narrow crowded streets, and our driver began to shout at the rickshaws and pedestrians in our path. As we approached the vegetable market, Uncle Philip suddenly rapped his cane to make the carriage stop.

9   "From here, we'll go on foot," he said to me. "I know a good short cut. It'll be much quicker."

10   This made perfectly good sense. I knew from experience how the little streets off Nanking Road could become so clogged with people that a carriage or motor car would often not move for five, even ten minutes at a time. I thus allowed him to help me down from the carriage with no argument. But it was then, I recall, that I had my

first presentiment that something was wrong. Perhaps it was something in Uncle Philip's manner. But then he smiled and made some remark I did not catch in the noise around us. He pointed towards a nearby alley and I stayed close behind him as we pushed our way through the good-humoured throng. We moved from bright sun to shade, and then he stopped and turned to me, right there in the midst of the jostling crowd. Placing a hand on my shoulder, he asked:

11   "Christopher, do you know where we are now? Can you guess?"

12   I looked around me. Then pointing towards a stone arch under which crowds were pressing around the vegetable stalls, I replied: "Yes. That's Kiukiang Road through there."

13   "Ah. So you know exactly where we are." He gave an odd laugh. "You know your way around here very well."

14   I nodded and waited, the feeling rising from the pit of my stomach that something of great horror was about to unfold. Perhaps Uncle Philip was about to say something else—perhaps he had planned the whole thing quite differently—but at that moment, as we stood there jostled on all sides, I believe he saw in my face that the game was up. A terrible confusion passed across his features, then he said, barely audibly in the din:

15   "Good boy."

16   He grasped my shoulder again and let his gaze wander about him. Then he appeared to come to a decision I had already anticipated.

17   "Good boy!" he said, this time more loudly, his voice trembling with emotion. Then he added: "I didn't want you hurt. You understand that? I didn't want you hurt."

18   With that he spun round and vanished into the crowd. I made a half-hearted effort to follow, and after a moment caught sight of his white jacket hurrying through the people. Then he had passed under the arch and out of my view.

19   For the next few moments I remained standing there in the crowd, trying not to pursue the logic of what had just occurred. Then suddenly I began to move, back in the direction we had just come, to the street in which we had left the carriage. Abandoning all sense of decorum, I forced my way through the crowds, sometimes pushing violently, sometimes squeezing myself through gaps, so that people laughed or called angrily after me. I reached the street to discover of course that the carriage had long since gone on its way. For a few confused seconds I stood in the middle of the street, trying to form in my head a map of my route back home. I then began to run as fast as I could.

20   I set off at a run down that long road, and even though I soon began to pant pathetically, even though the heat and exhaustion reduced me at times to little more than walking pace, I believe I did not stop at all.

21   I knew as soon as I turned through our gateway—though there was nothing obvious to tell me so—that I was too late. I found the front door bolted. I ran to the back door, which opened for me, and ran through the house shouting.

22   The house appeared to be empty. And I knew, as I had known throughout that punishing run home, that my mother was gone.

Adapted from the novel *When We Were Orphans* by Kazuo Ishiguro

[END OF PASSAGE]

[BLANK PAGE]

FOR OFFICIAL USE

C

Total
Mark

0860/406

NATIONAL
QUALIFICATIONS
2009

FRIDAY, 8 MAY
2.30 PM – 3.20 PM

**ENGLISH
STANDARD GRADE**
Credit Level
Reading
Questions

Fill in these boxes and read what is printed below.

Full name of centre

Town

Forename(s)

Surname

Date of birth
Day   Month   Year   Scottish candidate number   Number of seat

**NB   Before leaving the examination room you must give this booklet to the invigilator.
If you do not, you may lose all the marks for this paper.**

Marks

QUESTIONS

Write your answers in the spaces provided.

Look at Paragraphs 1 and 2.

1. "I had been able to relax for a while" (Paragraph 1)

    (*a*)   Why was Christopher able to relax?

    _____   2   1   0

    (*b*)   What does the expression "for a while" suggest about Christopher's usual state of mind?

    _____   2   ■   0

2. Write down an expression from Paragraph 2 which suggests that the family had been under strain for some time.

    _____   2   ■   0

Look at Paragraphs 3 to 6.

3. Uncle Philip seemed at first to be a generous and caring person.

    What evidence is there in this section that he was **both** generous and caring?

    _____

    _____   2   1   0

4. Christopher became very excited about Uncle Philip's plan.

    Give **three** ways in which the writer indicates Christopher's excitement in Paragraph 4.

    (i) _____

    (ii) _____

    (iii) _____   2   1   0

PAGE
TOTAL

Marks

5. Why do you think Christopher was delighted to hear his mother laugh? (Paragraph 4)

_____

_____   2 1 0

6. Explain the function of the dashes in ". . . this very atmosphere—this feeling that things were perhaps starting to return to what they had been—which played . . ." (Paragraph 4)

_____

_____   2 1 0

7. **In your own words**, explain what Christopher means by "lower my guard". (Paragraph 4)

_____

_____   2 ■ 0

8. Give **two** reasons why Christopher did not object to wearing a jacket.

(i) _____

(ii) _____   2 1 0

Look at Paragraph 7.

9. Give **two** pieces of evidence which might suggest that Uncle Philip was feeling tense.

(i) _____

(ii) _____   2 1 0

[Turn over

PAGE TOTAL

Marks

10. "But I thought nothing of it at the time" (Paragraph 7)

What does this statement suggest?

_____   2 ■ 0

Look at Paragraphs 8 and 9.

11. What explanation does Christopher suggest for his uncle's silences on their journey? (Paragraph 8)

Use your own words in your answer.

_____

_____   2 1 0

12. **In your own words**, explain how the writer indicates the changing surroundings along the route towards the city centre.

_____

_____   2 1 0

13. "From here, we'll go on foot . . ." (Paragraph 9)

From your reading of the passage as a whole, what was the real reason for Uncle Philip's decision to leave the carriage and start walking?

_____   2 ■ 0

Look at Paragraph 10.

14. Quote **three** examples of effective word choice used by the writer to describe the busy streets "off Nanking Road".

(i) _____

(ii) _____

(iii) _____   2 1 0

PAGE
TOTAL

Marks

15. "We moved from bright sun to shade" (Paragraph 10)

Why do you think the writer refers to **light** and **darkness** at this point in the passage?

_____

_____   2 1 0

Look at Paragraphs 14 to 17.

16. The writer describes the strong feelings experienced by both Christopher and Uncle Philip.

(*a*)   Quote **two** expressions which show Christopher's strong feelings.

_____

_____   2 1 0

(*b*)   Quote **two** expressions which show Uncle Philip's strong feelings.

_____

_____   2 1 0

17. Why did Uncle Philip repeat "I didn't want you hurt"? (Paragraph 17)

_____   2 ■ 0

[Turn over

PAGE
TOTAL

Marks

Look at Paragraph 19.

18. "Then suddenly I began to move . . ." (Paragraph 19)

    Comment on the writer's use of word choice **and** sentence structure in this paragraph to describe Christopher's journey back.

    (*a*) Word choice:

    _____

    _____   2 | 1 | 0

    (*b*) Sentence structure:

    _____

    _____   2 | 1 | 0

19. "all sense of decorum" (Paragraph 19)

    Tick (✓) the box beside the best definition of "decorum".

proper behaviour	
bad behaviour	
anxious behaviour	
aggressive behaviour	

    2 | ■ | 0

Look at Paragraph 20 to the end of the passage.

20. In Paragraph 20, the writer describes Christopher as physically tired but mentally determined. Give **one** piece of evidence showing he was tired and **one** piece of evidence showing his determination.

    _____

    _____   2 | 1 | 0

Marks

21. "I knew as soon as . . ." (Paragraph 21)

"I knew, as I had known . . ." (Paragraph 22)

Why does the writer repeat "I knew" in this way?

_____   2 ■ 0

Think about the passage as a whole.

22. Explain what you think happened to Christopher's mother.

Support your answer by referring to evidence from the passage.

Explanation _____

_____

Evidence _____

_____   2 1 0

[END OF QUESTION PAPER]

FOR OFFICIAL USE

p2	
p3	
p4	
p5	
p6	
p7	
TOTAL MARK	

FOR OFFICIAL USE

STANDARD GRADE | GENERAL

2010

READING

[BLANK PAGE]

G

0860/403

NATIONAL QUALIFICATIONS 2010	THURSDAY, 29 APRIL 1.00 PM – 1.50 PM	**ENGLISH STANDARD GRADE** General Level Reading Text

Read carefully the passage overleaf. It will help if you read it twice. When you have done so, answer the questions. Use the spaces provided in the Question/Answer booklet.

CHIMPS GO APE IN ZOO

Ricky, Kindia, Quarzeh and all the rest—meet the chimpanzees who are now hanging out in Edinburgh's new plush £5·6 million property.

1   Ricky is munching slowly on the yellow of a hard-boiled egg, staring at the funny-looking fellow-primate on the other side of the glass. The 47-year-old chimpanzee once travelled the high seas on a merchant navy ship. Today he looks content, if slightly tired by the adventures of his youth. Crouching to introduce myself, I feel the urge to make small talk. "Hello Ricky . . . erm . . . enjoying your lunch?" He pauses, lifts an eyebrow in a recognisably snooty gesture, before turning to the more pressing business of scooping out the white of the egg from its cracked shell.

2   Ricky and the 10 other chimps at Edinburgh Zoo have every reason to feel a little superior. They have just moved into a state-of-the-art, air-conditioned, £5·6 m luxury pad. Budongo Trail, which opens officially this weekend, is the largest chimpanzee enclosure in the world, and offers Ricky and his friends a higher standard of living than most humans will ever enjoy.

3   The complex is made up of three huge interconnected pods which open up into a gardened forest zone, complete with the longest, most intricate climbing frame ever built for apes. There's even a moat, which stops the water-shy chimps venturing too far, as well as adding to the sense of baronial splendour. Although the chimps are under observation, the place looks like too much fun to merit any comparison with the Big Brother house. It's more like a Crystal Maze set or the glamorous island hideaway of a James Bond baddie.

4   "They've moved from an ordinary house to a millionaire's mansion," beams Stephen Woollard, as he shows me round the place, justifiably proud of the structure he helped design. The education manager from the Royal Zoological Society of Scotland says the idea of a network that allowed scientists to study chimps in something like their natural environment was first proposed in the 1960s. He seems delighted this has finally been realised so spectacularly.

5   "Zoos have moved on from the old idea of looking at things lined up in cages, but we wanted to move it on further and set a whole new standard," he says. "It was something of a leap of faith, but the reaction has been tremendous. Everyone who sees the place says, 'Oh this is fantastic.'"

6   As we walk through the interactive exhibits, Woollard stops to explain how a cartoon game called Eddie Says, which lets children learn chimp gestures, was based on physical movements of none other than the zoologist himself. "Yes, they copied me, so I had to do all this sort of thing . . ." In an instant, Woollard becomes the perfect chimp, scrambling and hopping noisily around on the floor. "You see, it shouldn't be like a museum, where everything is hands-off. The kids will be running around, touching everything, as they should," he says.

7   Although the place appears to be one giant playground, the long glass frames of the enclosure pods also allow for serious study of animal behaviour. The project is linked to the conservation work of the Budongo Forest in north-west Uganda, where a team of researchers are gaining a better understanding of the threats faced by the forest's 600 or so chimpanzees. The population is falling because of habitat destruction and traps set for bush meat. The Royal Zoological Society of Scotland has been the primary sponsor of the African field station for the last three years, and many at Edinburgh Zoo have travelled there to gain further insight into chimp-life in the wild.

Characteristics of people

8   Laura McHugh is one of the lucky zoo-keeping researchers. The 23-year-old used her Ugandan adventure to learn how to differentiate between chimps. "It was amazing to see how the guys over there recognised each of the

chimps, knew their date of birth, and who was related to who," she enthuses. When McHugh came back to Scotland, it didn't take long to identify the zoo's residents. "You begin to recognise broad shoulders, say, or a slight beard. Now, to me, they have the characteristics of people."

9   The team at Budongo Trail cottoned on to the idea of giving the chimps celebrity status. There's Kindia, the boy-crazy teenager, and Lucy, the greedy guts of the gang. Visitors can even buy a glossy monthly magazine called Ape Vine!, packed full of the latest Budongo gossip. It's a good gimmick, but the personalities are far from manufactured. As we stare down into pod three, Quarzeh, the boisterous alpha male, is teaching nine-year-old Liberius how to tear up an egg carton. "It's too early to tell, but Liberius is potentially a future dominant male," McHugh explains. "He's still quite skinny though, so it's mostly just play-fights with his friend Kindia at the moment."

10   Ricky is also proving true to form as the loner with a shady past, eating lunch up on the glass window ledge, interacting with us rather than his hairy housemates. "Possibly because he was at sea, he does like being near humans," says McHugh. "But since coming to the Budongo Trail, he does engage in grooming a bit more." Professor Woollard concurs: "Yes,

he's had a bad start in life, and picked up some bad habits, but he's become more at ease."

Chimp culture

11   Staff say the apes are happier than ever before. The ceilings are four times as high as the zoo's previous enclosure, and even the soil is altered to copy the changing smells and textures of the wild. The sheer size of the place allows them freedom to separate in groups, spend time alone, or come together again to communicate.

12   "They do have the basics of language, and we're trying to discover what kind of level of language they have," Woollard explains. "It is possible there are many different dialects, since the dialect here in Edinburgh is different from chimps in Chester, or in Uganda. Do chimps have culture? We don't have all the answers." Chimp life reveals fresh marvels on a daily basis. Woollard believes visitors can help build a more complete behavioural picture by noting the quirks of the Budongo 11 as they go about their business. So, if you see Ricky when you visit Edinburgh Zoo, do say hello. The pleasantries might well have a purpose.

By Adam Forrest

[END OF PASSAGE]

[BLANK PAGE]

FOR OFFICIAL USE

Total
Mark

G

0860/404

NATIONAL
QUALIFICATIONS
2010

THURSDAY, 29 APRIL
1.00 PM – 1.50 PM

ENGLISH
STANDARD GRADE
General Level
Reading
Questions

Fill in these boxes and read what is printed below.

Full name of centre

Town

Forename(s)

Surname

Date of birth
Day   Month   Year   Scottish candidate number   Number of seat

**NB Before leaving the examination room you must give this booklet to the Invigilator.
If you do not, you may lose all the marks for this paper.**

SA 0860/404 6/57710

©

Marks

QUESTIONS

Write your answers in the spaces provided.

Look at Paragraphs 1 and 2.

1. Where exactly is the writer at the start of the passage?

    _____   2 1 0

2. In Paragraph 1, the writer makes Ricky the chimp seem human.

    Give **two** examples from Paragraph 1 of Ricky's "human" behaviour.

    (i) _____

    (ii) _____   2 1 0

3. In Paragraph 1, the writer introduces himself to Ricky.

    Describe Ricky's reaction when the writer speaks to him.

    _____

    _____   2 1 0

4. Give **three** reasons why, according to the writer, the chimps have "every reason to feel a little superior". (Paragraph 2)

    (i) _____

    (ii) _____

    (iii) _____   2 1 0

Look at Paragraphs 3 to 5.

5. Explain how the design of the "forest zone" (Paragraph 3) helps the chimps keep **both** active **and** safe.

    _____

    _____   2 1 0

PAGE
TOTAL

Marks

6. Write down **two** expressions from Paragraph 4 which show the contrast between the chimps' new enclosure and their old home.

2 ■ 0

7. Explain fully why the new enclosure is useful to scientists.

_____

_____

2 1 0

8. Stephen Woollard, the zoo's education manager, is both "proud" and "delighted" about the new enclosure. (Paragraph 4)

In your own words, explain why he is **both** "proud" **and** "delighted".

Proud _____

Delighted _____

2 1 0

Look at Paragraphs 6 and 7.

9. " . . . we walk through the interactive exhibits." (Paragraph 6)

Show how the idea of "interactive exhibits" is continued in this paragraph.

_____

_____

2 1 0

10. Which of the following expressions best sums up Stephen Woollard's attitude to the interactive exhibits? Tick (✓) **one** box.

Rather uninterested	
Very enthusiastic	
Slightly critical	

Give a reason from the passage to support your answer.

_____

2 1 0

PAGE
TOTAL

Marks

11. What evidence is there that the enclosure is part of a serious, international "study of animal behaviour"? (Paragraph 7)

_____

_____   2 1 0

12. **In your own words**, explain why the chimp population in Uganda is falling.

_____

_____   2 1 0

Look at Paragraphs 8 to 10.

13. ". . . differentiate between chimps." (Paragraph 8)

Tick (✓) the box beside the meaning of "differentiate between".

To study closely	
To help	
To relate to	
To tell apart	

2 ■ 0

14. The chimps have been given "celebrity status". (Paragraph 9)

(*a*) In what **two** ways are the chimps like human celebrities?

_____

_____   2 1 0

(*b*) Why do you think the team decided to give the chimps "celebrity status"?

_____

_____   2 ■ 0

PAGE
TOTAL

Marks

15. ". . . greedy guts of the gang."

". . . good gimmick." (Paragraph 9)

Identify the technique used in these expressions.

_____

2 ■ 0

16. **In your own words**, explain what we learn about Liberius' place in the chimp group.

_____

_____

2 1 0

17. Ricky's "bad start in life" had led to "some bad habits". (Paragraph 10)

(a) Give **one** example of Ricky's "bad habits".

_____

2 ■ 0

(b) How do we know that he is now "more at ease" with the other chimps?

_____

2 ■ 0

Look at Paragraphs 11 and 12.

18. ". . . the apes are happier than ever before." (Paragraph 11)

Give **three** reasons for this.

(i) _____

(ii) _____

(iii) _____

2 1 0

19. In Paragraph 12, Professor Woollard discusses the language of the chimps.

In your own words, explain what he means by "different dialects".

_____

_____

2 1 0

[Turn over

PAGE
TOTAL

Marks

20. "Chimp life reveals fresh marvels on a daily basis." (Paragraph 12)

Explain **in your own words** what the writer means by this.

_____

_____   2 1 0

21. How can visitors to the zoo help the scientists?

_____

_____   2 1 0

Think about the passage as a whole.

22. "CHIMPS GO APE IN ZOO"

Give **two** reasons why this is a suitable headline for this article.

(i) _____

(ii) _____   2 1 0

23. What is the main purpose of this passage? Tick (✓) the best answer.

To argue that animals like chimps should not be kept in zoos.	
To give a positive, informative view of the new enclosure.	
To request donations for the upkeep of the new enclosure.	

Give **one** piece of evidence from the passage to support your answer.

_____   2 1 0

[*END OF QUESTION PAPER*]

PAGE
TOTAL

FOR OFFICIAL USE

p2 ☐

p3 ☐

p4 ☐

p5 ☐

p6 ☐

TOTAL
MARK ☐

FOR OFFICIAL USE

[BLANK PAGE]

[BLANK PAGE]

C

0860/405

NATIONAL QUALIFICATIONS 2010	THURSDAY, 29 APRIL 2.30 PM – 3.20 PM	ENGLISH STANDARD GRADE Credit Level Reading Text

Read carefully the passage overleaf. It will help if you read it twice. When you have done so, answer the questions. Use the spaces provided in the Question/Answer booklet.

IN THE SILENCE

1   The stooks[1] of corn glimmered in the moonlight and boys' voices could be heard as they played hide and seek among them. How calm the night was, how stubbly the field! Iain crouched behind one of the stooks listening, watching for deepening shadows, his face and hands sweaty, his knees trembling with excitement. Then quite suddenly he heard the voices fading away from him, as if the boys had tired of their game and gone home, leaving him undetected. Their voices were like bells in the distance, each answering the other and then falling silent. He was alone.

2   The moonlight shimmered among the stooks so that they looked like men, or women, who had fallen asleep upright. The silence gathered around him, except that now and again he could hear the bark of a dog and the noise of the sea. He touched the stubble with his finger and felt it sharp and thorny as if it might draw blood. From where he was he could see the lights of the houses but there was no human shape to be seen anywhere. The moon made a white road across the distant sea.

3   He moved quietly about the field, amazed at the silence. No whisper of wind, no rustle of creature—rat or mouse—moving about. He was a scout on advance patrol, he was a pirate among his strawy treasure chests. If he thrust his hand into one, he might however find not gold but some small nocturnal animal. Very faintly he heard the soft throaty call of an owl. He was on a battlefield among the dead.

4   He began to count the stooks and made them twelve in all. It was a struggle for him for he was continually distracted by shadows and also not at all good at arithmetic, being only seven years old and more imaginative than mathematical. Twelve stooks set at a certain glimmering distance from each other. Twelve treasure chests. Twelve men of straw. He counted them again, and again he got twelve so he had been right the first time.

5   A cat slanted along in front of him, a mouse in its jaws, its eyes cold and green. The mouse's tail was dangling from its mouth like a shoelace. He put out his hand, but the cat quickly ran away from him towards its busy house, carrying its prey. Its green eyes were solid and beautiful like jewels.

6   He took a handkerchief from his pocket and began to dry his face. In the darkness he couldn't see the handkerchief clearly, it appeared as a vague ghostly shape, and though it had red spots on it he couldn't make them out. This was the quietest he had ever heard the world before. Even the cat had made no noise when it passed him. During the daytime there was always sound, but now even the dog had stopped barking. He could hear no sound of water, not any noise at all. He put his hand out in front of him and could see it only as a faint shape, as if it were separate from the rest of his body.

7   He looked up at the moon which was quite cold in the sky. He could see the dark spots on it and it seemed to move backwards into the sky as he looked. What an extraordinary calm was everywhere. It was as if he had been left in charge of the night, as if he was the only person alive, as if he must take responsibility for the whole world. No sound of footsteps could be heard from the road that lay between the wall and the houses.

8   The silence lasted so long that he was afraid to move. He formed his lips as if to speak but he didn't have the courage. It was as if the night didn't want him to speak, were forbidding him to do so, as if it were saying to him, This is my kingdom, you are not to do anything I don't wish you to do. He could no longer hear the noise of the sea, as if it too had been commanded to be quiet. It was like a yellow shield in the distance, flat and made of hammered gold.

[1] Tall bundles of corn tied together.

9   For the first time in his life he heard the beating of his own heart. Pitter patter it went, then it picked up power and became stronger, heavier. It was like a big clock in the middle of his chest. Then as quickly as it had started, it settled down again and he held his breath. The laden enchanted night, the strangeness of it. He would not have been surprised to see the stooks beginning to dance, a strawy dance, one which they were too serious to do in the daytime, when everyone was watching. He felt daring as well as frightened, that he should be the only one to stay behind, that he should be the dweller among the stooks. How brave he was and yet how unreal and ghostly he felt. It was as if the boys had left him and gone to another country, pulling the roofs over their heads and putting off the switch beside the bed.

10   This was the latest he had ever been out. He imagined himself staying there all night and the boys appearing to him in the morning, their faces red with the sun, shouting and screaming, like warriors. The sun was on their faces like war paint. They came out of their boxes pushing the lids up, and suddenly there they were among the stubble with their red knees and their red hands.

11   The stooks weren't all at the same angle to the earth. As he listened in the quietness he seemed to hear them talking in strawy voices, speaking in a sort of sharp, strawy language. They were whispering to each other, deep and rough and sharp. Their language sounded very odd, not at all liquid and running, but like the voice of stones, thorns. The field was alive with their conversation. Perhaps they were discussing the scythe that had cut them down, the boys that played hide and seek among them. They were busy and hissing as if they had to speak as much as possible before the light strengthened around them.

12   Then they came closer together, and the boys seemed suddenly very far away. The stooks were pressed against each other, composing a thorny spiky wall. He screamed suddenly and stopped, for at the sound the stooks had resumed their original positions. They were like pieces on a board. He began to count them again, his heart beating irregularly. Thirteen, where there had been twelve before. Where had the thirteenth come from?

13   He couldn't make out which was the alien one, and then counted them again and again. Then he saw it, the thirteenth. It was moving towards him, it had sharp teeth, it had thorny fingers. It was sighing inarticulately like an old woman, or an old man, its sigh was despairing and deep. Far beyond on the road he could sense that the boys were all gathered together, having got out of their boxes. They were sighing, everyone was sighing like the wind. Straw was peeling away from them as if on an invisible gale. And finally they were no longer there, but had returned to their boxes again and pulled the roofs over their heads.

14   He didn't notice the lights of the house go out as he walked towards the thirteenth stook, laid his head on its breast and fell asleep among the thorns.

Adapted from a short story by Iain Crichton Smith

[END OF PASSAGE]

[BLANK PAGE]

FOR OFFICIAL USE

C

Total Mark

0860/406

NATIONAL QUALIFICATIONS 2010

THURSDAY, 29 APRIL 2.30 PM – 3.20 PM

ENGLISH
STANDARD GRADE
Credit Level
Reading
Questions

Fill in these boxes and read what is printed below.

Full name of centre

Town

Forename

Surname

Date of birth

| Day | Month | Year | Scottish candidate number | | Number of seat |

NB Before leaving the examination room you must give this booklet to the Invigilator. If you do not, you may lose all the marks for this paper.

Marks

QUESTIONS

Write your answers in the spaces provided.

Look at Paragraph 1.

1. Explain exactly what Iain has been doing at the start of the story.

_____

_____ 2 1 0

2. In Paragraph 1, the writer suggests Iain's feeling of excitement. By referring to **one** example from Paragraph 1, explain how word choice is used to achieve this.

_____

_____ 2 1 0

3. Iain hears the voices of the other boys. **Quote** a simile which describes their voices. What does it suggest about their voices?

_____

_____ 2 1 0

4. "He was alone." (Paragraph 1)

    (a) Why is this an important moment in the story?

    _____ 2 ■ 0

    (b) Identify **one** way the writer shows it is important.

    _____ 2 ■ 0

Look at Paragraph 2.

5. What is missing from the scene around him?

    _____ 2 ■ 0

Marks

6. "The moon made a white road across the distant sea." (Paragraph 2)

(*a*) What technique is used in this expression?

_____   2 ■ 0

(*b*) Explain fully what this expression suggests about the moonlight.

_____

_____   2 1 0

Look at Paragraphs 3 and 4.

7. Explain the use of dashes in ". . . —rat or mouse— . . ." (Paragraph 3)

_____

_____   2 1 0

8. Paragraph 3 shows Iain's imagination working as he looks at the stooks of corn.
Give **two** examples from Paragraph 3 of things Iain imagines the stooks to be.

_____

_____   2 1 0

9. Give **two** reasons why Iain finds it difficult to count the stooks. **Use your own words** as far as possible.

_____

_____   2 1 0

10. Iain's attention is focussed on the stooks in Paragraph 4.

Identify **two** features of sentence structure used to convey his intense focus in Paragraph 4.

_____

_____   2 1 0

[Turn over

PAGE
TOTAL

Marks

Look at Paragraphs 5 and 6.

11. Iain watches a cat go past in Paragraph 5.

    Show how the writer uses the cat to add to the **beautiful** yet **menacing** qualities of the night.

    beautiful _____

    menacing _____   2 1 0

12. What **two** aspects of the night does the writer describe in Paragraph 6?

    _____

    _____   2 1 0

Look at Paragraphs 7 and 8.

13. Why does Iain feel he has "been left in charge of the night"?

    _____   2 ■ 0

14. Explain how word choice is used to indicate the power of the night.

    _____

    _____   2 1 0

Look at Paragraphs 9 to 11.

15. "The laden enchanted night . . ." (Paragraph 9)

    How does the writer continue this idea in Paragraph 9?

    _____   2 ■ 0

16. Iain thinks about the other boys appearing the next day.

    Identify **one** contrast between the moment of the boys' appearance and the night time.

    _____

    _____   2 ■ 0

PAGE TOTAL

Marks

17. ". . . he seemed to hear them talking . . ." (Paragraph 11)

By referring to the passage, identify and explain **one** technique the writer uses to describe the stooks' language.

_____

_____   2 | 1 | 0

Look at Paragraph 12.

18. Show how the writer conveys the idea that Iain feels threatened by the stooks.

_____

_____   2 | 1 | 0

19. Why does the writer use a question at the end of Paragraph 12?

_____   2 | ■ | 0

Look at Paragraphs 13 and 14.

20. Iain's experience becomes more dream-like in Paragraph 13.

(a) Show how the writer's description of the thirteenth stook adds to the feeling of nightmare.

_____

_____   2 | 1 | 0

(b) Show how the description of the other boys adds to the dream-like effect.

_____

_____   2 | 1 | 0

[Turn over

PAGE
TOTAL

Marks

Think about the passage as a whole.

21. Why might the reader be surprised by the final paragraph? (Paragraph 14)

_____

_____   2

22. Iain is a character who is highly imaginative and very young.

By referring closely to the passage, show how **both** of these aspects of his character are conveyed to the reader.

imaginative _____

young   _____   2   1

[END OF QUESTION PAPER]

PAGE
TOTAL

[BLANK PAGE]

FOR OFFICIAL USE

p2	
p3	
p4	
p5	
p6	
TOTAL MARK	

STANDARD GRADE | GENERAL

2011
READING

[BLANK PAGE]

G

0860/403

NATIONAL QUALIFICATIONS 2011	FRIDAY, 6 MAY 1.00 PM – 1.50 PM	ENGLISH STANDARD GRADE General Level Reading Text

Read carefully the passage overleaf. It will help if you read it twice. When you have done so, answer the questions. Use the spaces provided in the Question/Answer booklet.

In this passage the writer describes a childhood visit to Glasgow at Christmas.

BRIGHT LIGHTS
BIG CITY

1 Glasgow didn't have Christmas, it *was* Christmas. Even I knew that. A small-town seasider who would never swim, a child thrilled by beauty who somehow managed to break every glass ornament she ever touched, I knew the difference between magic and cold reality. Our town had miles of seaweed and pink rock with writing through it, cows and rolling greenery. We had industrial-strength downpours of rain. Glasgow people came to us in the summer holidays, desperate for sunburn, seagulls and seafood. But sea breezes and face-filing sand counted for nothing in winter. Nothing desirable, at least. At the opposite end of the year, as the dark descended, people wanted the city; for dazzle, the warmth of crowds and snowy shop displays. The place for cheer, therefore, was at the other end of the train line. Glasgow. My sister worked there in a stockbroker's office, typing important letters she did not understand, and claimed the city was what counted. "Our town is a dump," she'd say, rolling her eyes. "We've only a daft wee tree at the War Memorial. Glasgow's got hundreds. Lights and everything, George Square, you canny imagine it. Glasgow's the works!"

2 I got to see what those works were for the first time in December, 1961. I was five, and for the occasion dressed in a red Peter Pan collar coat and white nylon gloves.

3 "You've got to look nice for Santa," my mother said, scouring the side of my mouth with a spit-doused hankie till it hurt. "He lives up the stairs in the store," she explained, checking my face for further signs of imperfection, laziness and disease. The journey, it seemed, was putting us on show. "You keep they gloves on and mind they're new. One mark and you're for it, lady."

4 Whatever "it" was, I knew to steer clear.

5 The train was cold and the seats kitted out in dark, shiny tartan. An overhead rack hung like a hammock on a wooden frame, waiting for luggage. "Touch nothing," my mother said. "The windows are filthy." There was no arguing. Our view was strips of grass and passing branches, visible in glimpses through grime. Central Station, however, supplied the journey's missing sense of space. It was big enough for trains to roll right inside and from my vantage point, some three feet from the ground, high as cliffs. The noise of our footsteps over the platform shook waves into puddles as we passed. A bouquet of pigeons with rose-pink chests opened like roses. That was the size of the place: there were pigeons indoors, a clock the size of our bathroom. I tripped over my own feet, staring.

6   Outside, Glasgow presented itself: a black city. The buildings were coated with velvet-deep soot. There were charcoal-coloured statues at office doors or holding up second and third storeys of buildings. My mother hauled me by the hand down a long corridor of ash-grey walls and matching sky, my face brushing against the tweedy coats of strangers, to—my mother's words—the fanciest shop in the world. There was a Christmas tree inside the door, a sour reek of adult perfume. The grotto, three floors up, was a room full of glittery cotton wool and animal cut-outs, with a red-suited man in a squinty beard, the elastic of which stretched too far beneath his ears. I would not sit on his knee and my mother was embarrassed. When I resisted two shoves, she lifted me by the arms and sat me there, whether he or I liked it or not. Santa looked tired, and I felt uncomfortable. My failure to respond when asked what I wanted for Christmas did not throw him. It must have happened several times that day. He gave me my gift and released me back to the wild. The gift itself was a pink manicure set with sequins on the front. It had scissors and little metal sticks that looked like miniature butcher's tools. Whatever they were for, it was lovely. It took a moment to work out this was mine to keep. I did not need to hand it back for another little girl. The little pink cutlery set was mine.

7   We shared a vanilla ice cream in the store's café then stood on the stairs to see their display of lights and bells from above. "We're like angels," my mother said, her mouth pale now she'd eaten her lipstick off on a scone.

8   The food apart, nothing was bought. Odd though it seems now, in an age where people take day trips to shopping centres for pleasure, we had not come for the shopping. We had come for the promised lights, which we could not, according to my sister, imagine for ourselves. She was right. I remember still the eye-watering colour strung between high buildings, the never-ending sky with no stars. But the bit that took my breath away was entirely natural. It was starlings: thousands upon thousands of starlings in George Square, a chorus of birds clinging or swooping between telegraph wires, the reckless, nerve-shredding noise of screaming.

9   My mother had to pull me away to get the train. All the way back, I knew my sister was right. I would not have imagined any of it. But what was magic, what stayed with me and always would, was not the lights or the trees, not the manicure set from a man who was not Santa at all.

10   It was the birds. Little creatures making what life they could in the city square, singing for dear life and thriving. I'd never have imagined the courage, the grandeur of those birds. I got told off on the way home for making my gloves black, of course. I'd not get to go again. But it was worth it. In one visit and forever, the noise of a real chorus that has never lost its volume, its truth.

11   The starlings have long gone from George Square. No matter. First thing on Christmas morning, we go out feeding birds. It seems the right thing to do.

Adapted from a newspaper article by Janice Galloway

[END OF PASSAGE]

[BLANK PAGE]

FOR OFFICIAL USE

G

Total
Mark

0860/404

NATIONAL
QUALIFICATIONS
2011

FRIDAY, 6 MAY
1.00 PM – 1.50 PM

ENGLISH
STANDARD GRADE
General Level
Reading
Questions

Fill in these boxes and read what is printed below.

Full name of centre

Town

Forename(s)

Surname

Date of birth
Day   Month   Year   Scottish candidate number   Number of seat

NB Before leaving the examination room you must give this booklet to the Invigilator. If you do not, you may lose all the marks for this paper.

Marks

QUESTIONS

Write your answers in the spaces provided.

Look at Paragraph 1.

1. "Glasgow didn't have Christmas, it *was* Christmas." (Paragraph 1)

   What do you think the writer means by this?

   _____   2 ■ 0

2. Explain **one** of the two surprising things the writer tells us about herself.

   _____

   _____   2 1 0

3. ". . . sunburn, seagulls and seafood." (Paragraph 1)

   Identify the technique used here.

   _____   2 ■

4. Glasgow was more popular than the seaside in the winter. Give **three** things Glasgow could offer in winter that the writer's town could not.

   (i) _____

   (ii) _____

   (iii) _____   2 1 0

5. Write down **one** thing the writer's sister **did** and **one** thing she **said** which showed her view of her town.

   _____

   _____   2 1 0

PAGE
TOTAL

Marks

Look at Paragraphs 2 to 4.

6. Give **two** details which show that preparing to travel to Glasgow was not pleasant for the writer.

    _____

    _____   2 1 0

7. "Whatever "it" was, I knew to steer clear." (Paragraph 4)

    In what way does the writer make this statement stand out?

    _____   2 ■ 0

Look at Paragraph 5.

8. **In your own words**, explain what spoiled the view out of the train window on the way to Glasgow.

    _____

    _____   2 1 0

9. "Central Station, however, supplied the journey's missing sense of space." (Paragraph 5)

    Give **two** ways in which the writer shows the "space" of Central Station.

    _____

    _____   2 1 0

10. "A bouquet of pigeons with rose-pink chests opened like roses." (Paragraph 5)

    (*a*) Identify **two** techniques used here.

    _____   2 1 0

    (*b*) Explain what the pigeons are doing.

    _____   2 ■ 0

[Turn over

PAGE TOTAL

Marks

Look at Paragraph 6.

11. ". . . a black city." (Paragraph 6)

    How does the writer continue this idea in Paragraph 6?

    _____

    _____   2 | 1 | 0

12. Give **one** piece of evidence which shows that the streets were crowded.

    _____   2 | ■ | 0

13. Explain the use of the dashes in the expression "–my mother's words–". (Paragraph 6)

    _____

    _____   2 | 1 | 0

14. **In your own words**, explain why the Santa costume was not convincing.

    _____

    _____   2 | 1 | 0

15. What did the writer's mother do to make her sit on "Santa's" knee?

    _____

    _____   2 | 1 | 0

16. Write down **two** expressions which show the writer's confusion about what the gift was.

    _____

    _____   2 | 1 | 0

PAGE TOTAL

Marks

17. **In your own words**, explain fully how the writer felt about receiving the gift.

_____

_____   2 1 0

Look at Paragraphs 7 and 8.

18. In what way were the writer and her mother "like angels"?

_____   2 ■ 0

19. What was "odd" about the shopping trip?

_____   2 ■ 0

20. Explain fully why the starlings made such an impression on the writer when she first saw them.

_____

_____

_____   2 1 0

Read Paragraph 9 to the end of the passage.

21. Give **two** pieces of evidence from Paragraph 9 which show the writer really enjoyed this outing.

_____

_____   2 1 0

22. "But it was worth it." (Paragraph 10)

Why was the writer in trouble on the way home and why was it "worth it"?

_____

_____   2 1 0

[Turn over

PAGE
TOTAL

Marks

23. The visit made a lasting impression on the writer. In what way does she show this in Paragraph 11?

_____   2 1 0

Think about the passage as a whole.

24. Do you think the writer gives a realistic description of this childhood experience?

Give **one** piece of evidence from the passage to support your answer.

Yes	
No	

_____

_____   2 ■ 0

[END OF QUESTION PAPER]

PAGE
TOTAL

FOR OFFICIAL USE

p2	
p3	
p4	
p5	
p6	
TOTAL MARK	

[0860/404]

[BLANK PAGE]

STANDARD GRADE | CREDIT

2011
READING

[BLANK PAGE]

C

0860/405

NATIONAL
QUALIFICATIONS
2011

FRIDAY, 6 MAY
2.30 PM – 3.20 PM

ENGLISH
STANDARD GRADE
Credit Level
Reading
Text

Read carefully the passage overleaf. It will help if you read it twice. When you have done so,
answer the questions. Use the spaces provided in the Question/Answer booklet.

BOUNCING OFF WALLS

An underground phenomenon involving running through cities and leaping over obstacles, parkour is the epitome of cool for its growing army of fans. Critics say it's stupidly dangerous. Kenneth Stephen hits the streets to hear both sides of the story.

1   It is a Wednesday night in Glasgow. The high walls, rails and steps of Rottenrow Gardens look like some form of municipal amphitheatre under the reddening sky. Several athletic youths in T-shirts and jogging bottoms are moving quickly. They bound over rocks, sure-footed, before leaping like cats into the air, their trainers crunching into the gravel on landing. To move off again, they roll on to their shoulders on the hard ground, springing up and pushing off in one fluid, unbroken movement. You can still see dust in the air as they pass on through the shadows, up and over a wall or vaulting a railing.

2   Witnessing this for the first time, you might think you've come across an unorthodox piece of urban theatre, and in a sense you have. This is parkour, an underground activity that started in the suburbs of Paris in the 1980s and is now sweeping Europe, fuelled by the Internet, especially DIY productions on video sharing websites.

3   Participants are known as traceurs (or traceuses for females) and the parks and city structures of Scotland are rapidly becoming their stage. "I really like the ability to move the way you want, rather than being bound by the way the street designer wanted you to move," says Glynn Forsythe, 24, one of the traceurs assessing the obstacles dotting the campus of Strathclyde University. The biology PhD student points to a walkway snaking into the distance. "It might be faster to go across that railing than take the path. I like that," he says. "It makes things interesting."

4   Like its more expressive cousin free running, parkour is a street art that embraces continuous movement over obstacles. There are no rules and no projected outcomes; parkour simply advocates that individuals "find their own way". The aim is to improve strength, both mental and physical, while developing your technique to overcome ever-greater barriers. The obstructions can be bollards, benches, scaffolding, advertising boards, bins, cars, bus stops or high walls. In extreme cases, they can be whole buildings.

5   In 2002, a BBC trailer titled *Rush Hour* depicted the French founder of parkour, David Belle, now 35, leaping between the rooftops of urban buildings 200 feet above street level. It is dynamic images such as these that have lured youngsters out of their bedrooms into public spaces.

6   Documentaries such as Channel 4's *Jump London* (2003) and its sequel *Jump Britain* (2005) followed. Assisted by the reach and immediacy of the Internet, parkour spread. It was featured in films such as *District 13* and *Casino Royale*, and now sports clothing firms have jumped on the bandwagon, using parkour's hip factor to sell clothes and trainers.

7   Back in Glasgow, it's only the grey tower blocks on the skyline and the cranes of the Clyde shipyards that remind you this isn't a Paris backstreet or downtown New York. Parkour, say its practitioners, transgresses physical, mental, cultural and geographical boundaries. It is unique, operates off the radar and involves risk and a sense of danger. Just as city kids of the late 1970s and early 1980s found creativity in skate parks and hip-hop, it isn't difficult to see why, for some, parkour is now synonymous with freedom and cool.

8   Therein lies the problem, though. The glamourisation of parkour has been a catalyst for its growth but has also communicated mixed messages. The explosion in popularity has caused a schism to develop within the parkour community over the movement's philosophy. Is it, for example, about dangerous jumps across tenements, and the sort of flips and tricks which have seen brand-name executives reaching for their cheque books? Or is it, as many argue, about fine-tuning the mind and body to overcome obstacles and fear?

9   Whenever accidents happen, parkour is inevitably labelled as a dangerous fringe activity with little place in modern towns and cities. According to the Glasgow traceurs, the media backlash against the activity has been disproportionate. They feel the headlines ignore the spirit of positivity which Belle and others, such as *Jump Britain's* Sebastien Foucan, brought to the activity.

10   "*Jump Britain* got us started," says Chris Grant of Glasgow Parkour Coaching, as he takes a short break from leading the traceurs through conditioning work. He is currently Scotland's only professional parkour coach. "We were all young and in the same boat. But the documentary was the best thing and the worst thing to happen to parkour. It popularised it but it was also responsible for a lot of misconceptions."

11   Grant, 25, takes a quick gulp of mineral water, his eyes still focusing on the figures stretching on the pavement. Behind them, draped on a mock arch, is a banner reading Glasgow, Commonwealth Games 2014.

12   Getting the public and civic authorities to look behind the sensationalism to find parkour's beating heart is something with which Glasgow's serious traceurs have tasked themselves. For them, the increased profile of parkour counts for little if it doesn't lead to a proportionate level of acceptance. They feel the best way to understand the activity is to watch it being practised, and encourage doubters to come along and witness proceedings for themselves.

13   "Just because people don't understand it, that doesn't mean it's wrong," stresses Grant, before leading the traceurs over a water feature beside red-brick walls. Watching the traceurs learn to cushion a footfall properly or break a jump, it is difficult to question the merits of the activity. Strength, concentration, practice and technique are all in evidence. In a society that persistently bemoans childhood obesity and risk-averse behaviour, these are perhaps qualities to be coveted, not derided.

14   Grant, a graduate in music and computing from the University of Glasgow, got into parkour with a friend in 2005. Working in Glasgow bars, they found the activity was the perfect way to exercise after closing time. "There was always a quiet spot where you wouldn't get moved on," he recalls. "It fitted in well with our lifestyle at the time because we would always be up until about three in the morning anyway." After his initial dalliance, Grant trained with the French originators of parkour before bringing his knowledge back to Glasgow. He trains every day, whether in the activity's more physical aspects or in its technique. More than 100 people attend his adults and female-only classes every week. In 2007, he collaborated with the National Theatre of Scotland for its production *Bolt*, which included elements of parkour. He has also coached children at three local schools. All three have requested further sessions.

15   In the 18 months since he founded Glasgow Parkour Coaching, assisted by fellow coaches Mick McKeen, Gavin Watson and David Lang, Grant says he has seen only one injury. "It happened over there," he says, pointing to a row of innocuous wooden posts. In front of him, traceurs and traceuses from tonight's class are poised like trapeze artists on railings completing a study in balance. "The main problem for us is bureaucracy and the persistent idea that this is a dangerous activity," says Grant. "People think parkour is just about jumping off walls and they have trouble seeing the outcomes and rewards. We have liability insurance—we do risk assessments and we get people to sign disclaimers. We are serious about what we do. I don't sleep sometimes because, as a coach, I am responsible for other people."

16   One of the revealing things about watching Grant's mixed-adult class in action is the demographic make-up of the group. Besides the likes of University of Glasgow students in their twenties, Grant has coached physics teachers and seen people as old as 50 practising parkour regularly. Since *Casino Royale* hit cinema screens, parkour's training methods have been incorporated into the battle drills of the British Royal Marines.

17   "People shouldn't just see this as hopping off walls, because it is much more," says Angie Rupp, a 31-year-old vet from Munich who is studying neuroscience in Glasgow. She began practising parkour after reading about it in a magazine article last May. "Parkour requires conditioning and the use of the mind," she says. "It makes any risk a calculated risk, like driving a fast car. We live in such a cotton wool society, but with parkour you are constantly assessing how far you can go and pushing your limits just a wee bit further each time. It helps me to assess problems, and I take the determination needed for parkour into my everyday life." Joining Rupp on a network of scaffolding adjoining two university buildings is Kate Cohen, a 21-year-old finance student. The pair complete a sideways traverse with the same ease as their three male counterparts. Neither of them appears even remotely out of breath, despite the strength required to pull their body weight across the hanging bars. "You must be fit and strong and make sure you use the right technique," says Cohen. "It can look very dangerous, big or impressive—but when you start learning, it's not like that at all."

18   As the traceurs and traceuses pull on their zipped tops and make for their homes across the city, the banner for Glasgow 2014 is almost blanked out by the creeping darkness. Their hobby will maybe never be accepted as a Commonwealth sport, but if they can continue to chip away at the misconceptions, at the very least they might have more places to train without being moved on. That would be progress.

Adapted from an article from
The Herald Magazine

[END OF PASSAGE]

[BLANK PAGE]

FOR OFFICIAL USE

C

Total
Mark

0860/406

NATIONAL
QUALIFICATIONS
2011

FRIDAY, 6 MAY
2.30 PM – 3.20 PM

ENGLISH
STANDARD GRADE
Credit Level
Reading
Questions

Fill in these boxes and read what is printed below.

Full name of centre   Town

Forename(s)   Surname

Date of birth
  Day   Month   Year   Scottish candidate number   Number of seat

NB Before leaving the examination room you must give this booklet to the Invigilator. If you do not, you may lose all the marks for this paper.

Marks

QUESTIONS

Write your answers in the spaces provided.

Look at Paragraphs 1 and 2.

1. "It is a Wednesday night in Glasgow." (Paragraph 1)

    Why do you think the writer begins the article with this information?

    _____   2 ■ 0

2. Comment on the writer's use of **word choice** to show the agility of the "athletic youths".

    _____

    _____   2 1 0

3. ". . . unorthodox piece of urban theatre . . ." (Paragraph 2)

    In your own words, explain what this means.

    _____   2 1 0

Look at Paragraphs 3 and 4.

4. **Using your own words as far as possible**, give **three** reasons why parkour appeals to Glynn Forsythe.

    _____

    _____

    _____   2 1 0

5. ". . . a walkway snaking into the distance." (Paragraph 3)

    Identify the technique used in this expression and explain why it is appropriate.

    _____

    _____   2 1 0

PAGE
TOTAL

Marks

6. ". . . to overcome ever-greater barriers." (Paragraph 4)

    How does the writer develop this idea in the rest of the paragraph?

    _____

    _____   2 1 0

Look at Paragraphs 5 to 8.

7. **In your own words**, explain the impact of the trailer *Rush Hour*.

    _____

    _____   2 1 0

8. (a) What evidence is there in Paragraphs 6 and 7 of the growing popularity of parkour?

    _____

    _____   2 1 0

    (b) **In your own words**, explain fully why people enjoy taking part in parkour.

    _____

    _____   2 1 0

9. "Therein lies the problem, though." (Paragraph 8)

    Explain how this sentence acts as a link between Paragraphs 7 and 8.

    _____

    _____   2 1 0

10. ". . . a catalyst for its growth . . ." (Paragraph 8)

    In your own words, explain what "catalyst" means in this expression.

    _____

    _____   2 ■ 0

[Turn over

PAGE
TOTAL

Marks

11. **Using your own words as far as possible**, explain the **two** different views of parkour outlined in Paragraph 8.

_____

_____   2 1

Look at Paragraphs 10 to 13.

12. Chris Grant describes *Jump Britain* as "the best thing and the worst thing" to happen to parkour. (Paragraph 10)

    In your own words explain:

    (a) why it was "the best thing"?

    _____   2 ■

    (b) why it was "the worst thing"?

    _____   2 ■

13. What do "Glasgow's serious traceurs" (Paragraph 12) aim to achieve?

    Explain **one** way in which they hope to achieve their aim.

    _____

    _____   2 1

14. Which description best sums up the writer's reaction, as he watches the traceurs train? Tick (✓) **one** box.

Concerned, in case they injure themselves.	
Jealous, because they are so talented.	
Admiring, because they show skill and care.	
Dismissive, because it is a worthless activity.	

2 ■

PAGE TOTAL

Marks

15. From Paragraph 13, describe **two** ways in which parkour could help society.

_____

_____   2 1 0

Look at Paragraphs 14 and 15.

16. What evidence is there of the success of both Chris Grant's adult **and** school classes?

_____

_____   2 1 0

17. Comment on the writer's use of the word "innocuous" to describe the wooden posts in Paragraph 15.

_____

_____   2 1 0

18. ". . . poised like trapeze artists . . ." (Paragraph 15)

Identify the technique used in this expression and explain why it is appropriate.

_____

_____   2 1 0

19. "The main problem for us is bureaucracy." (Paragraph 15)

Show how the context helps you understand the meaning of "bureaucracy".

Meaning _____

Context _____   2 1 0

[Turn over

PAGE
TOTAL

Marks

Look at Paragraph 16 to the end of the passage.

20. How does the writer illustrate "the demographic make-up of the group"? (Paragraph 16)

_____

_____   2   1

21. Why do you think the writer includes the interview with Angie Rupp?

_____   2   ■

22. **In your own words**, explain **one** way that parkour can have a wider impact on life, according to Angie Rupp.

_____

_____   2   ■

Think about the passage as a whole.

23. Tick (✔) the box beside the statement which you think best sums up what parkour is all about.

Pushing yourself mentally and physically.	
Allowing anyone to achieve great things.	
Being an individual is important in modern society.	

By referring closely to the passage, give **two** pieces of evidence to support the choice you have made.

_____

_____   2   1

[END OF QUESTION PAPER]

PAGE TOTAL

FOR OFFICIAL USE

p2 ☐

p3 ☐

p4 ☐

p5 ☐

p6 ☐

TOTAL
MARK ☐

[BLANK PAGE]

STANDARD GRADE | GENERAL

2012
READING

[BLANK PAGE]

G

0860/29/11

NATIONAL QUALIFICATIONS 2012	THURSDAY, 26 APRIL 1.00 PM – 1.50 PM	ENGLISH STANDARD GRADE General Level Reading Text

Read carefully the passage overleaf. It will help if you read it twice. When you have done so, answer the questions. Use the spaces provided in the Question/Answer booklet.

THREE MEN AND A DOG

You don't need to lug a tent on a long-distance walk in the Lakes. Kevin Rushby and his two sons discover barn camping on a rite of passage hike with their young hound.

1   It's so easy when they're puppies. You stroll down the street and they come home exhausted. People stop and have conversations.

2   "Aren't you gorgeous?" (That can be disappointing, of course: it's the dog who is being addressed, not you). Then they get bigger. They want proper walks. They want sticks thrown. We got a mongrel terrier pup from a rescue centre. And when Wilf reached full size, I started looking to take him for a decent walk in deep countryside—a rite of passage for a young hound, somewhere beyond the realm of the dreaded poo bin. There were two teenage sons too, Con and Niall, and they seemed surprisingly enthusiastic—there's one tip for getting your kids to walk: buy or borrow a dog.

3   The Lake District seemed a good choice—plenty of wonderful walking there—but with snow on the way I didn't fancy camping. Instead, I booked us into a couple of barns. There's a whole slew of them across the Lakes, offering varying degrees of comfort from downright basic to . . . well, let's call it cosily austere. Nevertheless, they did seem to offer a cushier alternative to tents.

4   Our hotel in Keswick was willing to take a dog for a night in one of their dog-friendly rooms, so we planned on a comfortable start followed by three days of walking in a great horseshoe around the southern extremities of Borrowdale.

5   I have this fond vision of dogs in hotels and pubs. It's an affable labrador-type creature laid out under the table, snoozing. At the hotel, Wilf isn't like that. He runs riot. He loves hotels. He loves the way people drop crisps in the bar. He sneaks into a neighbour's room and sniffs their luggage for food. Curiously, they laugh indulgently and say things like, "You're a lovable chap, aren't you?" A dog's life doesn't seem so bad, really. Wilf soon settles down on his dedicated luxury bed and sleeps like a baby. I spend the night half-awake, stirring at every doggy snort, worrying that he'll get up and cock his leg on the four-poster. Mercifully that doesn't happen.

6   At first light, we set out. Winter walking means every hour of daylight is precious. We soon leave Keswick behind and climb steadily on to the ridge of High Seat. The weather forecast is for snow showers, but all we get is mist and cloud and occasional tantalising glimpses of Derwent Water below. On Bleaberry Fell, Wilf disappears for 10 minutes and I fear he will return with one of the black grouse that are chuckling at us from afar (not a sheep, we took the precaution of stock-training him before the trip, and anyway he would look silly as he's only knee-height to a ewe). He eventually reappears, grouseless, bounding across clumps of heather as if he's on springs.

7   We eat our lunch looking down at Watendlath, perhaps the most idyllic of Lakeland settings. Then we march down to Rosthwaite in Borrowdale and search out our first barn.

8   The barn is a beautiful old stone Cumbrian longhouse set on the side of a meadow close to Stonethwaite Beck. Downstairs is a kitchen with microwave, kettle and trestle tables; upstairs is a room with foam mattresses. Sadly there are no straw bales or lambs bleating in cribs: it's all very well-swept.

9   We sleep pretty well. Next morning we bemoan the recent, and permanent, closure of the shop in Rosthwaite—breakfast and lunch will finish all our food supplies.

10   The walk up to Dale Fell takes our minds off this logistical problem: first with all the old slate-mine workings, a fascinating bit of industrial history, then with marvellous views as we hit the ridge, heading west. Far away to our right, across a pack of fells, disappearing in mist, is the Solway Firth; to our left, Morecambe Bay with its wind farms.

11   By the time we drop down into the village of Buttermere, we are tired but happy. It's been a great day's walk. Wilf must have once again done 40 miles to our 10. We are ready to sample either of the two pubs. Our hopes, however, are dashed: both are shut. Recent floods in Cumbria have caused such a dearth of customers that midweek closures have come into force. Cragg Barn is 100 yards up the lane and looks cold. There are snow clouds overhead. Inside is a kitchen —sink and table—then an upstairs sleeping room with foam mattresses wrapped in industrial black plastic. No heating. This is definitely the spartan end of the camping barn experience, and the only food we have is a can of tripe and turkey in gravy, which Wilf refuses to share.

12   There is no mobile coverage so we find a phone box and ring for a taxi. Twenty quid to get back to Keswick for fish and chips; then 20 more to return. If you choose your barn for its proximity to a pub I recommend checking opening times.

13   The final day, and it's the big one. Snow clouds are hovering over Whiteless Breast, our first fell. The views are brief and brilliant: a few seconds of long vistas across sunlight dappled sea to the Isle of Man, swiftly gone. Wilf goes up the slope at top speed and disappears into the cloud, snapping wildly at the first snow flurries of his short life; flurries that are thickening into a white out. We reach the top of Whiteless Pike. I wonder if anyone ever called Mountain Rescue because their dog got lost. At that moment he reappears, only to pursue a snowflake down a steep slope then—horror—over the edge. We all stop.

14   "Is that a cliff?" asks Con. With visibility at a few metres, it's impossible to tell. The steep grassy bank is slick with ice and snow. I take a couple of tentative steps down. It would be very easy to lose control and slide.

15   At that moment, Wilf scrabbles back over the brink, looking a bit shaken. He bounds back to us, but stays close after that.

16   Conditions are now quite testing. A rising cold wind is driving icy snow into our faces. We push on. This was definitely the rite of passage I had wanted for all my young hounds, but would I be up to it myself? Good trips always have that moment of uncertainty: should we go on? Is it safe?

17   One last challenge is rerouting due to a bridge being washed away, then we are on the path into Keswick where we meet a fellow walker and dog expert who looks Wilf up and down.

18   "Aren't you gorgeous? You're a fell terrier, aren't you?"

19   Wilf seemed to prick up his ears. He was a breed. He was meant to be. We have covered 30 miles and climbed 7,500 feet, but he had done in excess of 100 miles, and, I reckon, scaled a Mount Everest in height. He trotted into Keswick with his tail up, an acknowledged fell terrier. The rest of us were perky also, but in a less demonstrative way. The rite of passage had worked. We were fell terriers, too.

Adapted from an article in
"Saturday Guardian"

[END OF PASSAGE]

[BLANK PAGE]

FOR OFFICIAL USE

Total Mark

G

0860/29/01

NATIONAL
QUALIFICATIONS
2012

THURSDAY, 26 APRIL
1.00 PM – 1.50 PM

ENGLISH
STANDARD GRADE
General Level
Reading
Questions

Fill in these boxes and read what is printed below.

Full name of centre

Town

Forename(s)

Surname

Date of birth

Day   Month   Year   Scottish candidate number   Number of seat

NB Before leaving the examination room you must give this booklet to the Invigilator. If you do not, you may lose all the marks for this paper.

Marks

QUESTIONS

Write your answers in the spaces provided.

Look at Paragraphs 1 and 2.

1. "It's so easy when they're puppies." (Paragraph 1)

   What, according to the writer, is "easy" about caring for a puppy?

   _____   2

2. Why is it more difficult to care for an older, bigger dog?

   Use your own words in your answer.

   _____

   _____   2   1

Look at Paragraphs 3, 4 and 5.

3. ". . . well, let's call it . . ." (Paragraph 3)

   What style of language is the writer using in this expression?

   _____   2

4. Describe the writer's "vision" of how dogs should behave in pubs and hotels.

   Use your own words in your answer.

   _____

   _____   2   1

5. "Wilf isn't like that." (Paragraph 5)

   What does Wilf do that isn't "like that"?

   (i) _____

   (ii) _____

   (iii) _____   2   1

PAGE
TOTAL

Marks

6. Do the other guests object to Wilf's behaviour? Tick (✓) **one** box.

Yes	
No	

Write down an expression which supports your answer.

_____   2 | 1 | 0

7. Identify the contrast between the way Wilf and his owner pass the night in the hotel.

_____

_____   2 | 1 | 0

Look at Paragraphs 6 and 7.

8. Why is every hour of daylight "precious"? (Paragraph 6)

_____

_____   2 | ■ | 0

9. Give **two** reasons why the sheep should be safe from Wilf.

_____

_____   2 | 1 | 0

10. Explain how the writer's word choice creates a clear picture of Wilf's behaviour in Paragraph 6.

_____

_____   2 | 1 | 0

[Turn over

PAGE
TOTAL

Marks

Look at Paragraphs 8 and 9.

11. Identify **three** positive features of the first barn.

(i) _____

(ii) _____

(iii) _____   2 1 0

12. Explain fully the problem they face the next morning.

_____

_____   2 1 0

Look at Paragraphs 10, 11 and 12.

13. In what way does the writer contrast the past and the present in Paragraph 10?

_____

_____   2 1 0

14. Explain **in your own words** the change of mood they experience when they arrive in Buttermere.

_____

_____   2 1 0

15. Give **two** reasons why Cragg Barn is an uncomfortable place.

_____

_____   2 1 0

Marks

16. The walkers have problems with food in Paragraphs 11 and 12.

    (*a*) Why do they not eat the only tinned food they have left?

    _____   2 ■ 0

    (*b*) Describe the difficulties they face getting fish and chips.

    _____   2 | 1 | 0

Look at Paragraphs 13, 14 and 15.

17. The views are "brief and brilliant". (Paragraph 13)

    Identify the technique used in this expression.

    _____   2 ■ 0

18. "Snow clouds are hovering . . ." (Paragraph 13)

    How does the writer show the changing weather conditions in this part of the walk?

    (i) _____

    (ii) _____

    (iii) _____   2 | 1 | 0

19. At the end of Paragraph 13, how does the writer use word choice **and** sentence structure to show their panic when Wilf disappears?

    Word choice _____

    Sentence structure _____   2 | 1 | 0

[Turn over

PAGE
TOTAL

Marks

20. Which word is closest in meaning to "tentative"?   (Paragraph 14)

Tick (✓) **one** answer.

Hurried	
Cautious	
Panicking	
Terrified	

2

Look at Paragraph 16 to the end of the passage.

21. "Conditions are now quite testing." (Paragraph 16)

How does the writer continue this idea later in the passage?

_____

_____   **2**   **1**

22. Explain fully why Wilf "seemed to prick up his ears". (Paragraph 19)

_____

_____   **2**   **1**

23. Why did the writer feel positive about his family's **and** Wilf's achievements on the walk?

_____

_____   **2**   **1**

PAGE TOTAL

Think about the passage as a whole.

24. What seems to be the main purpose of the passage? Tick (✓) **one** box.

To criticise barn camping.	
To give information about the Lake District.	
To describe the challenges they faced on their trip.	

Give **one** piece of evidence to support the answer you have chosen.

_____

2 1 0

[END OF QUESTION PAPER]

Marks

PAGE
TOTAL

FOR OFFICIAL USE

p2	☐
p3	☐
p4	☐
p5	☐
p6	☐
p7	☐
TOTAL MARK	☐

FOR OFFICIAL USE

STANDARD GRADE | CREDIT

2012
READING

[BLANK PAGE]

C

0860/31/11

NATIONAL
QUALIFICATIONS
2012

THURSDAY, 26 APRIL
2.30 PM – 3.20 PM

ENGLISH
STANDARD GRADE
Credit Level
Reading
Text

Read carefully the passage overleaf. It will help if you read it twice. When you have done so, answer the questions. Use the spaces provided in the Question/Answer booklet.

This passage is taken from the introduction to a book about how we make quick decisions about important things.

The Statue That Didn't Look Right

1   In September of 1983, an art dealer by the name of Gianfranco Becchina approached the J. Paul Getty Museum in California. He had in his possession, he said, a marble statue dating from the sixth century BC. It was what is known as a kouros – a sculpture of a male youth standing with his left leg forward and his arms at his sides. There are only about two hundred kouroi in existence, and most have been recovered badly damaged or in fragments from grave sites or archaeological digs. But this one was almost perfectly preserved. It stood close to seven feet tall. It had a kind of light-coloured glow that set it apart from other ancient works. It was an extraordinary find. Becchina's asking price was just under $10 million.

2   The Getty moved cautiously. It took the kouros on loan and began a thorough investigation. Was the statue consistent with other known kouroi? The answer appeared to be yes. [...] Where and when had the statue been found? No one knew precisely, but Becchina gave the Getty's legal department a sheaf of documents relating to its more recent history. ...

3   A geologist from the University of California named Stanley Margolis came to the museum and spent two days examining the surface of the statue with a high-resolution stereomicroscope. He then removed a core sample from ... just below the right knee and analysed it using an electron microscope, electron microprobe, mass spectrometry, X-ray diffraction, and X-ray fluorescence. The statue was made of dolomite marble from the ancient Cape Vathy quarry on the island of Thasos, Margolis concluded, and the surface of the statue was covered in a thin layer of calcite — which was significant, Margolis told the Getty, because dolomite can turn into calcite only over the course of hundreds, if not thousands, of years. In other words, the statue was old. It wasn't some contemporary fake.

4   The Getty was satisfied. Fourteen months after their investigation of the kouros began, they agreed to buy the statue. In the autumn of 1986, it went on display for the first time. The *New York Times* marked the occasion with a front-page story. ...

5   However, the kouros had a problem. It didn't look right. The first to point this out was an Italian art historian named Federico Zeri. ... When Zeri was taken down to the museum's restoration studio to see the kouros in December of 1983, he stared at the sculpture's fingernails. In a way he couldn't immediately articulate, they seemed wrong to him. Evelyn Harrison was next. She was one of the world's foremost experts on Greek sculpture, and she was in Los Angeles visiting the Getty. ... "Arthur Houghton, who was then the curator, took us down to see it," Harrison remembers. "He swished the cloth off the top of it and said,

'Well, it isn't ours yet, but it will be in a couple of weeks.' And I said, 'I'm sorry to hear that.'" What did Harrison see? She didn't know. In that very first moment, when Houghton swished off the cloth, all Harrison had was a hunch, an instinctive sense that something was amiss. A few months later, Houghton took Thomas Hoving, the former director of the Metropolitan Museum of Art in New York, to see the statue. Hoving always makes a note of the first word that goes through his head when he sees something new, and he'll never forget what that word was when he first saw the kouros. "It was 'fresh' – 'fresh,'" Hoving recalls. And "fresh" was not the right reaction to have to a two-thousand-year-old statue. Later, thinking back on that moment, Hoving realized why that thought had popped into his mind: "I had dug in Sicily, where we found bits and pieces of these things. They just don't come out looking like that. The kouros looked like it had been dipped in the very best caffè latte from Starbucks."

6   Hoving turned to Houghton. "Have you paid for this?"

7   Houghton, Hoving remembers, looked stunned.

8   "If you have, try to get your money back," Hoving said. "If you haven't, don't."

9   The Getty was getting worried, so they convened a special symposium on the kouros in Greece. They wrapped the statue up, shipped it to Athens, and invited the country's most senior sculpture experts. This time the chorus of dismay was even louder.

10   … Georgios Dontas, head of the Archaeological Society in Athens, saw the statue and immediately felt cold. "When I saw the kouros for the first time," he said, "I felt as though there was a glass between me and the work" […] Another expert thought it was a fake. Why? Because when he first laid eyes on it, he said, he felt a wave of "intuitive repulsion." By the time the symposium was over, the consensus among many of the attendees appeared to be that the kouros was not at all what it was supposed to be. The Getty, with its lawyers and scientists and months of painstaking investigation, had come to one conclusion, and some of the world's foremost experts in Greek sculpture — just by looking at the statue and sensing their own "intuitive repulsion" — had come to another. Who was right?

11   For a time it wasn't clear. […] But then, bit by bit, the Getty's case began to fall apart. The letters the Getty's lawyers used to carefully trace the kouros, turned out to be fakes. […] And what of the scientific analysis that said that the surface of the Getty kouros could only have aged over many hundreds or thousands of years? Well, it turns out things weren't that cut and dried. Upon further analysis, another geologist concluded that it might be possible to "age" the surface of a dolomite marble statue in a couple of months using potato mould. In the Getty's catalogue, there is a picture of the kouros, with the notation "About 530 BC, or modern forgery."

12   When Federico Zeri and Evelyn Harrison and Thomas Hoving and Georgias Dontas — and all the others — looked at the kouros and felt an "intuitive repulsion," they were absolutely right. In the first two seconds of looking — in a single glance — they were able to understand more about the essence of the statue than the team at the Getty was able to understand after fourteen months. […] They simply took a look at that statue and some part of their brain did a series of instant calculations, and before any kind of conscious thought took place, they *felt* something. For Thomas Hoving, it was the completely inappropriate word "fresh" that suddenly popped into his head. In the case of one expert, it was a wave of "intuitive repulsion." For Georgios Dontas, it was the feeling that there was a glass between him and the work. Did they know why they knew? Not at all. But they *knew*.

13   The part of our brain that leaps to conclusions like this is called the adaptive unconscious, and the study of this kind of decision making is one of the most important new fields in psychology. [...]

14   Whenever we meet someone for the first time, whenever we interview someone for a job, whenever we react to a new idea, whenever we're faced with making a decision quickly and under stress, we use the adaptive unconscious. How long, for example, does it take you to decide how good your teacher is? A class? Two classes? A term? The psychologist Nalini Ambady once gave students three ten-second videotapes of a teacher — with the sound turned off — and found they had no difficulty at all coming up with a rating of the teacher's effectiveness. Then Ambady cut the clips back to five seconds, and the ratings were the same. They were remarkably consistent even when she showed the students just *two* seconds of videotape. Then Ambady compared those snap judgements of teacher effectiveness with evaluations of those same teachers made by their students after a full term of classes, and she found that they were also essentially the same. A person watching a silent two-second video clip of a teacher he or she has never met will reach conclusions about how good that teacher is that are very similar to those of a student who has sat in the teacher's class for an entire term. That's the power of our adaptive unconscious.

15   You may have done the same thing, whether you realized it or not, when you first picked up this article. Aren't you curious about what happened in those two seconds? [...]

Adapted from "Blink" by Malcolm Gladwell

[END OF QUESTION PAPER]

C

FOR OFFICIAL USE

Total Mark

0860/31/01

NATIONAL QUALIFICATIONS 2012

THURSDAY, 26 APRIL 2.30 PM – 3.20 PM

ENGLISH
STANDARD GRADE
Credit Level
Reading
Questions

Fill in these boxes and read what is printed below.

Full name of centre

Town

Forename(s)

Surname

Date of birth

Day	Month	Year	Scottish candidate number	Number of seat

NB Before leaving the examination room you must give this booklet to the Invigilator. If you do not, you may lose all the marks for this paper.

SA 0860/31/01 6/36510

Marks

QUESTIONS

Write your answers in the spaces provided.

Look at Paragraph 1.

1. What was the art dealer's aim when he approached the J. Paul Getty Museum?

    _____   2 ■

2. "He had in his possession, he said, a marble statue dating from the sixth century BC." (Paragraph 1)

    What does the expression "he said" add to the meaning of the sentence?

    _____   2 ■

3. "It was an extraordinary find." (Paragraph 1)

    (*a*) Quote the words which show the contrast between this kouros and most others.

    _____

    _____   2 1

    (*b*) Give **two** other reasons why the find was "extraordinary".

    _____

    _____   2 1

Look at Paragraphs 2 and 3.

4. "The Getty moved cautiously." (Paragraph 2)

    How does the rest of the paragraph continue this idea?

    _____

    _____   2 1

5. What details suggest that the geologist's tests were thorough?

    _____

    _____   2 1

PAGE TOTAL

Marks

6. Explain why the "thin layer of calcite" was "significant". **Use your own words** as far as possible.

_____

_____   2 1 0

Look at Paragraphs 4 to 8.

7. Why does the writer mention the "front-page story" in the "New York Times"? (Paragraph 4)

_____   2 ■ 0

8. "However, the kouros had a problem." (Paragraph 5)

   Show how this sentence acts as a link between Paragraphs 4 and 5.

_____

_____   2 1 0

9. Federico Zeri could not "immediately articulate" what was wrong with the statue. Explain **in your own words** what this means.

_____   2 1 0

10. ". . . seemed wrong . . ." (Paragraph 5)

    Quote an expression from later in Paragraph 5 which has a similar meaning.

_____   2 ■ 0

11. "He swished the cloth off the top of it . . ." (Paragraph 5)

    (*a*) What technique is used in this expression?

    _____   2 ■ 0

    (*b*) What does "swished" suggest about the way the cloth was removed?

    _____   2 1 0

[Turn over

PAGE
TOTAL

Marks

12. Explain why "fresh" was "not the right reaction to the statue".

_____ 2 1

13. Explain how Hoving's experience led him to feel that the statue looked wrong. **Use your own words** as far as possible.

_____

_____ 2 1

14. What is the effect of the writer's use of direct speech in Paragraphs 6 to 8?

_____ 2 ■

Look at Paragraphs 9 to 11.

15. ". . . convened a special symposium . . ." (Paragraph 9)

Show how the context helped you understand the meaning of "symposium".

_____

_____ 2 1

16. Show how the metaphor ". . . a wave of intuitive repulsion" (Paragraph 10) is an effective description of the expert's reaction to the statue.

_____

_____ 2 ■

17. **In your own words** explain the contrast between the Getty's investigation and the reaction of the experts in Paragraph 10.

_____

_____ 2 1

PAGE
TOTAL

Marks

Look at Paragraph 12.

18. "... — in a single glance — ..." (Paragraph 12)

    Comment on the writer's use of dashes in this expression.

    _____

    _____   2 | 1 | 0

19. "Did they know why they knew? Not at all. But they *knew*." (Paragraph 12)

    Identify and explain **two** techniques used in these sentences.

    (i) _____

    (ii) _____   2 | 1 | 0

Look at Paragraph 13 to the end of the passage.

20. **Using your own words** as far as possible, explain when we use the "adaptive unconscious".

    _____   2 | ■ | 0

21. "... ten-second videotapes . . . five seconds . . . just two seconds . . ." (Paragraph 14)

    Comment on the writer's use of time in these expressions.

    _____

    _____   2 | 1 | 0

22. **Using your own words**, explain fully what Nalini Ambady's research showed about students' views of teachers.

    _____

    _____   2 | 1 | 0

[Turn over

PAGE TOTAL

Marks

Think about the passage as a whole.

23. Explain fully how the final paragraph forms an effective conclusion to the passage.

_____

_____   2   1

[END OF QUESTION PAPER]

PAGE
TOTAL

FOR OFFICIAL USE

p2 ☐

p3 ☐

p4 ☐

p5 ☐

p6 ☐

TOTAL
MARK ☐

FOR OFFICIAL USE

[BLANK PAGE]

STANDARD GRADE | FOUNDATION | GENERAL | CREDIT

2008
WRITING

[BLANK PAGE]

**F
G
C**

0860/407

NATIONAL
QUALIFICATIONS
2008

TUESDAY, 6 MAY
9.00 AM – 10.15 AM

ENGLISH
STANDARD GRADE
Foundation, General
and Credit Levels
Writing

Read This First

1   Inside this booklet, there are photographs and words.
    Use them to help you when you are thinking about what to write.
    Look at all the material and think about all the possibilities.

2   There are 22 assignments altogether for you to choose from.

3   Decide which assignment you are going to attempt.
    Choose only **one** and write its number in the margin of your answer book.

4   Pay close attention to what you are asked to write.
    Plan what you are going to write.
    Read and check your work before you hand it in.
    Any changes to your work should be made clearly.

FIRST **Look at the picture opposite.**
It shows a car in heavy rain and hail.

NEXT Think about the dangers of extreme weather.

> WHAT YOU HAVE TO WRITE

1. **Write a short story** using the following opening:

   The car skidded violently. He struggled to regain control. Close to panic, he wrenched the steering wheel to the right . . .

   You should develop **setting** and **character** as well as **plot**.

   OR

2. What's going on with our weather?

   Individuals need to take steps to tackle climate change.

   Give your views.

   OR

3. Journeys can take unexpected turns.

   Write about an occasion when this happened to **you**.

   Remember to include your **thoughts and feelings**.

[Turn over

Page four

FIRST   **Look at the picture opposite.**
It shows young people together in a school cafeteria.

NEXT   Think about school experiences.

> WHAT YOU HAVE TO WRITE

4. A Best Friend Should Be . . .

    Write about the ideal qualities of a best friend.

    OR

5. Youth culture. There's no such thing.

    Give your views.

    OR

6. **Write about** an occasion when your loyalty to a friend was pushed to the limit.

    Remember to include your **thoughts and feelings**.

    OR

7. **Write a short story** using the following title:

    The School Gate.

    You should develop **setting** and **character** as well as **plot**.

    [Turn over

FIRST **Look at the picture opposite.
It shows a man staring.**

NEXT Think about being observed.

WHAT YOU HAVE TO WRITE

8. Big Brother is Watching You!

   Write about an occasion when you felt that there was no escape from authority.

   Remember to include your **thoughts and feelings**.

   OR

9. **Write a short story** using **ONE** of the following titles:

   Seeing is Believing   Close Up

   You should develop **setting** and **character** as well as **plot**.

   OR

10. All You Need is an Audience.

    The media give young people the idea that success comes easily.

    Give your views.

[Turn over

FIRST **Look at the picture opposite.**
It shows a boy with his grandfather.

NEXT Think about the positive relationship you have with an older relative.

> WHAT YOU HAVE TO WRITE

11. **Write about** an occasion when you learned a valuable lesson from an older relative.

    Remember to include your **thoughts and feelings**.

    OR

12. **Write a short story** using the following opening:

    Those were the moments he loved most. Grandpa reading to him with that lilting voice telling stories of . . .

    You should develop **setting** and **character** as well as **plot**.

    OR

13. We do not give the older generation the respect they deserve.
    Give your views.

    OR

14. **Write in any way you choose** using the picture opposite as your inspiration.

[Turn over

FIRST **Look at the picture opposite.
It shows an aircraft in the sunset.**

NEXT Think about air travel.

WHAT YOU HAVE TO WRITE
---

15. The damage to the environment caused by aircraft outweighs the advantages of cheap air travel.

    Give your views.

    OR

16. **Write a short story** using **ONE** of the following titles:

    A New Beginning   Touchdown

    You should develop **setting** and **character** as well as **plot**.

    OR

17. **Write in any way you choose** using the picture opposite as your inspiration.

[Turn over for assignments 18 to 22 on *Page twelve*

There are no pictures for these assignments.

18. **Write an informative article** for your school magazine titled:

    Technology: the impact on my education.

    OR

19. Nowadays there is less freedom of choice.

    Give your views.

    OR

20. **Write a short story** with the following opening:

    Beth stared again at the square glow from the computer screen in disbelief. She was going to be reunited with her sister at long last. She could hardly wait . . .

    You should develop **setting** and **character** as well as **plot**.

    OR

21. Education is about what we learn both **inside** and **outside** the classroom.

    Give your views.

    OR

22. **Describe the scene** brought to mind by **ONE** of the following:
    EITHER

    Snow fell, the flimsiest drops of geometric perfection, lightly, gently onto the village rooftops.

    OR

    With merciless rage, the sun scorched the earth to brittle hardness.

[END OF QUESTION PAPER]

STANDARD GRADE | FOUNDATION | GENERAL | CREDIT

2009
WRITING

[BLANK PAGE]

**F
G
C**

0860/407

NATIONAL
QUALIFICATIONS
2009

FRIDAY, 8 MAY
9.00 AM – 10.15 AM

ENGLISH
STANDARD GRADE
Foundation, General
and Credit Levels
Writing

Read This First

1 Inside this booklet, there are photographs and words.
    Use them to help you when you are thinking about what to write.
    Look at all the material and think about all the possibilities.

2 There are 21 assignments altogether for you to choose from.

3 Decide which assignment you are going to attempt.
    Choose only **one** and write its number in the margin of your answer book.

4 Pay close attention to what you are asked to write.
    Plan what you are going to write.
    Read and check your work before you hand it in.
    Any changes to your work should be made clearly.

FIRST   **Look at the picture opposite.**
         It shows a statue overlooking a city.

NEXT   Think about life in a city.

WHAT YOU HAVE TO WRITE

1. **Write about an occasion** when you went on a school trip to a city.

   Remember to include your **thoughts and feelings**.

   OR

2. Holidays are not just about sun, sea and sand.

   Give your views.

   OR

3. **Write a short story** using the following opening:

   From a great height he watched. Cars, buses, boats, people. Slowly, he drew his plans . . .

   You should develop **setting** and **character** as well as **plot**.

   OR

4. **Write in any way you choose** using the picture opposite as your inspiration.

[Turn over

FIRST **Look at the pictures opposite.**
They show people involved in different sports.

NEXT Think about what sport means to you.

| WHAT YOU HAVE TO WRITE |
---

5. My Sporting Hero.

   Write a magazine article giving information about your favourite sportsperson.

   OR

6. There should be more opportunities for sport in local communities.

   Give your views.

   OR

7. **Write a short story** using the title:

   Against the Odds

   You should develop **setting** and **character** as well as **plot**.

   OR

8. **Write about** a sporting occasion when taking part was more important than winning.

   Remember to include your **thoughts and feelings**.

[Turn over

FIRST   **Look at the picture opposite.**
             It shows a tigress and her cubs.

NEXT   Think about protecting animals.

WHAT YOU HAVE TO WRITE

---

9. One of the Family.

    Write about the importance of a pet in your life.

    Remember to include your **thoughts and feelings**.

    OR

10. **Write a magazine article** in which you present the case **for** the protection of an animal in danger.

    OR

11. **Write a short story** using **ONE** of the following titles:

    The Animal Kingdom   Animal Magic

    You should develop **setting** and **character** as well as **plot**.

    [Turn over

FIRST   **Look at the picture opposite.**
               It shows a man at the top of a staircase.

NEXT   Think about achievements in your life.

WHAT YOU HAVE TO WRITE

---

12. **Write about** an occasion when you achieved a personal goal after a struggle.

    Remember to include your **thoughts and feelings**.

    OR

13. Achievement in school is about more than success in exams.
    Give your views.

    OR

14. **Write a short story** using the following opening:

    It had been tough. Sacrifice. Time. Effort. Now she had succeeded. Let the new life begin . . .

    You should develop **setting** and **character** as well as **plot**.

                                                        [Turn over

FIRST   **Look at the picture opposite.**
               It shows two people on a survival course.

NEXT   Think about outdoor activities.

WHAT YOU HAVE TO WRITE

---

15. **Write about** an occasion when you learned new skills through taking part in an outdoor activity.

    Remember to include your **thoughts and feelings**.

    OR

16. **Write a short story** using the following title:

    Trapped in the Forest

    You should develop **setting** and **character** as well as **plot**.

    OR

17. Outdoor education should be available to all pupils.

    Give your views.

    [Turn over for assignments 18 to 21 on *Page twelve*

There are no pictures for these assignments.

18. **Describe the scene** brought to mind by **ONE** of the following:

    Light as air, they hovered then swooped, twisting impossibly around feather clouds.

    OR

    Waves lapped at pebbles on the distant shore and a kindly sun drew a gentle haze over the land.

19. Holidays at home are better for the environment than going abroad.

    Give your views.

    OR

20. **Write about** an occasion when you were a positive role model for a friend or relative.

    Remember to include your **thoughts and feelings**.

    OR

21. **Write a short story** using the following title:

    Paradise Lost

    You should develop **setting** and **character** as well as **plot**.

[END OF QUESTION PAPER]

STANDARD GRADE | FOUNDATION | GENERAL | CREDIT

2010
WRITING

[BLANK PAGE]

F G C

0860/407

NATIONAL
QUALIFICATIONS
2010

THURSDAY, 29 APRIL
9.00 AM – 10.15 AM

ENGLISH
STANDARD GRADE
Foundation, General
and Credit Levels
Writing

Read This First

1   Inside this booklet, there are photographs and words.
     Use them to help you when you are thinking about what to write.
     Look at all the material and think about all the possibilities.

2   There are 21 assignments altogether for you to choose from.

3   Decide which assignment you are going to attempt.
     Choose only **one** and write its number in the margin of your answer book.

4   Pay close attention to what you are asked to write.
     Plan what you are going to write.
     Read and check your work before you hand it in.
     Any changes to your work should be made clearly.

SA 0860/407 6/57710

FIRST **Look at the picture opposite.**
It shows a woman on a skateboard being helped by an expert.

NEXT Think about new challenges.

WHAT YOU HAVE TO WRITE

---

1. **Write a short story** using the title:

   The Rebel

   You should develop **setting** and **character** as well as **plot**.

   OR

2. We all have hidden talents.

   Education should be about discovering our strengths, not our weaknesses.

   Give your views.

   OR

3. **Write about** an occasion when you had an experience that changed your life.

   Remember to include your **thoughts and feelings**.

   OR

4. Look on the Bright Side!

   We need to have a more positive outlook on life.

   Give your views.

FIRST **Look at the picture opposite.
It shows an example of street art.**

NEXT Think about expressing yourself.

WHAT YOU HAVE TO WRITE

---

5. Graffiti: art or vandalism?

   Give your views.

   OR

6. **Write about** an occasion when breaking a rule was more important than following it.

   Remember to include your **thoughts and feelings**.

   OR

7. **Write a short story** using the title:

   The Smile

   You should develop **setting** and **character** as well as **plot**.

[Turn over

FIRST   **Look at the picture opposite.**
                  It shows a fairground at night.

NEXT   Think about the attraction of fairgrounds.

WHAT YOU HAVE TO WRITE

---

8. **Write a short story** using the following opening:

   Sal awakened slowly. Dazed at first, she tried to focus but she was still dizzy from the rollercoaster. At last, her eyes fixed on the empty booth, then beyond to the empty stalls and the empty fairground . . .

   You should develop **setting** and **character** as well as **plot**.

   OR

9. Entertainment today is too expensive for many young people.

   Give your views.

   OR

10. Fun for Everyone!

    Describe your favourite fairground attraction.

    Remember to include your **thoughts and feelings**.

[Turn over

FIRST   **Look at the pictures opposite.**
         They show images of Scotland.

NEXT   Think about living in Scotland.

WHAT YOU HAVE TO WRITE

11. **Write about** an occasion when you took part in a Scottish celebration or festival.

    Remember to include your **thoughts and feelings**.

    OR

12. **Write an article** for your school magazine in which you argue the case either **for** or **against** an independent Scotland.

    OR

13. **Write a short story** using the following opening:

    From the darkness, a glimmering light sparked faintly and began to glow . . .

    You should develop **setting** and **character** as well as **plot**.

                                                    [Turn over

FIRST   **Look at the picture opposite.**
         It shows two long shadows.

NEXT   Think about darkness and light.

WHAT YOU HAVE TO WRITE

---

14. **Write a short story** using the following opening:

    Something just wasn't right. He turned. Nothing. He turned again to see the outline of a dark figure . . .

    You should develop **setting** and **character** as well as **plot**.

    OR

15. Always in their Shadow!

    Write about an occasion when you felt second best.

    Remember to include your **thoughts and feelings**.

    OR

16. **Write in any way you choose** using the picture opposite as your inspiration.

[Turn over for assignments 17 to 21 on *Page twelve*

There are no pictures for these assignments.

17. **Describe the scene** brought to mind by **one** of the following:

Rain stained the still warm path; each collision a hiss.

OR

Slowly the sun dawned on an endless golden land.

OR

18. **Write an article** for your school magazine **describing** a visit to an unusual or interesting building.

OR

19. **Write about** an occasion when you were given good advice but did not take it.

Remember to include your **thoughts and feelings**.

OR

20. **Write a short story** using the following title:

The Arrival

OR

21. Learning to drive. Managing your money. Parenting.

What life skills would you like to learn at school?

[END OF QUESTION PAPER]

STANDARD GRADE | FOUNDATION | GENERAL | CREDIT

2011
WRITING

[BLANK PAGE]

F G C

0860/407

NATIONAL
QUALIFICATIONS
2011

FRIDAY, 6 MAY
9.00 AM – 10.15 AM

ENGLISH
STANDARD GRADE
Foundation, General
and Credit Levels
Writing

Read This First

1   Inside this booklet, there are photographs and words.
Use them to help you when you are thinking about what to write.
Look at all the material and think about all the possibilities.

2   There are 20 assignments altogether for you to choose from.

3   Decide which assignment you are going to attempt.
Choose only **one** and write its number in the margin of your answer book.

4   Pay close attention to what you are asked to write.
Plan what you are going to write.
Read and check your work before you hand it in.
Any changes to your work should be made clearly.

FIRST   **Look at the picture opposite.**
               It shows an anxious young man on his mobile phone.

NEXT   Think about difficult situations.

WHAT YOU HAVE TO WRITE

1. **Write a short story** using the following opening:

    Life was wonderful. Just great. Paul didn't have a care in the
    world. It was then that the phone rang . . .

    You should develop **setting** and **character** as well as **plot**.

    OR

2. **Write about** an occasion when **you** had a telephone call giving
    you unwelcome news.

    Remember to include your **thoughts and feelings**.

    OR

3. Stress. Stress. Stress. It's all we seem to hear these days.

    Some stress is actually good for people.

    Give your views.

[Turn over

[0860/407]

FIRST **Look at the picture opposite.**
It shows a boat in a storm.

NEXT Think about risks and dangers.

| WHAT YOU HAVE TO WRITE |

---

4. **Write a short story** using **one** of the following titles:

   Overboard   The Boat

   You should develop **setting** and **character** as well as **plot**.

   OR

5. Everyday life is full of risks. We can't avoid them.

   We simply need to accept that life is a risk.

   Give your views.

   OR

6. **Write about** an occasion when you took a memorable journey by boat.

   Remember to include your **thoughts and feelings**.

   OR

7. **Write in any way you choose** using the picture opposite as your inspiration.

[Turn over

FIRST **Look at the picture opposite.**
It shows a science lesson.

NEXT Think about science and technology.

> WHAT YOU HAVE TO WRITE

8. It is important that all pupils study science at school.
   Give your views.

   OR

9. **Write a short story** using **one** of the following titles:

   The Experiment   The Monster

   You should develop **setting** and **character** as well as **plot.**

   OR

10. **Write about** an occasion when science **or** technology changed your life.

    Remember to include your **thoughts and feelings**.

[Turn over

FIRST **Look at the picture opposite.**
It shows a bookshop.

NEXT Think about the importance of reading.

WHAT YOU HAVE TO WRITE
---

11. **Write a short story** using the following opening:

    She entered and walked to the back of the shop. She counted the bookshelves. One. Two. Three. This was it. She removed the book. And found herself in . . .

    You should develop **setting** and **character** as well as **plot.**

    OR

12. Reading books on a screen will never replace the good old-fashioned paperback.

    Give your views.

    OR

13. Curled up in front of the fire with a good book. Perfect.

    Write about the pleasure reading gives **you**.

    Remember to include your **thoughts and feelings.**

[Turn over

FIRST **Look at the picture opposite.**
It shows children playing at sunset.

NEXT Think about childhood memories.

WHAT YOU HAVE TO WRITE

14. **Write about** an occasion when you enjoyed a childhood pleasure.
Remember to include your **thoughts and feelings.**

OR

15. **Write a short story** using the title:

Sunset

You should develop **setting** and **character** as well as **plot**.

OR

16. **Write in any way you choose** using the picture opposite as your inspiration.

[Turn over for assignments 17 to 20 on *Page twelve*

There are no pictures for these assignments.

17. **Describe the scene** brought to mind by **one** of the following:

    EITHER

    Ice. Endless blue ice for a hundred miles in any direction. Sharp, cold, beautiful.

    OR

    Gold. Endless golden fields stretching and swaying in gentle winds to the far horizons.

    OR

18. **Write a description** of your local park.

    OR

19. We need more green spaces in cities.
    Give your views.

    OR

20. **Write a short story** using the title:
    Escape from the City
    You should develop **setting** and **character** as well as **plot**.

[END OF QUESTION PAPER]

[BLANK PAGE]

F G C

0860/32/01

NATIONAL
QUALIFICATIONS
2012

THURSDAY, 26 APRIL
9.00 AM – 10.15 AM

**ENGLISH
STANDARD GRADE**
Foundation, General
and Credit Levels
Writing

Read This First

1   Inside this booklet, there are photographs and words.
    Use them to help you when you are thinking about what to write.
    Look at all the material and think about all the possibilities.

2   There are 23 assignments altogether for you to choose from.

3   Decide which assignment you are going to attempt.
    Choose only **one** and write its number in the margin of your answer book.

4   Pay close attention to what you are asked to write.
    Plan what you are going to write.
    Read and check your work before you hand it in.
    Any changes to your work should be made clearly.

FIRST   **Look at the picture opposite.**
                 It shows a man surrounded by gadgets.

NEXT   Think about our need for possessions.

WHAT YOU HAVE TO WRITE

1. Our lives today are too cluttered. The pressure on us to buy new things increases daily.

   Give your views.

   OR

2. Buy. Buy. Buy.

   Write about an occasion when you felt the need to buy something new.

   Remember to include your **thoughts and feelings**.

   OR

3. **Write a short story** using the following title:

   The Treasure Hunt

   You should develop **setting** and **character** as well as **plot**.

[Turn over

FIRST   **Look at the picture opposite.**
It shows an old, ruined house.

NEXT   Think about the effects of time passing.

WHAT YOU HAVE TO WRITE

4. **Write a description** of the scene suggested by the picture opposite.

   OR

5. There are many lessons we can learn from the past.
   Give your views.

   OR

6. **Write about** an occasion when you made a fresh start.
   Remember to include your **thoughts and feelings**.

   OR

7. **Write an informative article** for your school magazine in which you describe a visit to a place of historic interest.

[Turn over

FIRST   **Look at the picture opposite.**
It shows a violinist.

NEXT   Think about performing.

WHAT YOU HAVE TO WRITE
---

8. **Write about** the importance of musical performance to **you**.

    Remember to include your **thoughts and feelings**.

    OR

9. **Write a short story** using the following opening:

    She caught her breath, then anxiously took to the stage. Blinding light. Deafening applause. She began . . .

    You should develop **setting** and **character** as well as **plot**.

    OR

10. Becoming really good at something always involves hard work.
    Give your views.

[Turn over

Image taken from www.bigfoto.com

FIRST   **Look at the picture opposite.**
It shows people playing in the snow.

NEXT   Think about winter.

WHAT YOU HAVE TO WRITE

---

11. Unexpected Fun.

    Write about an occasion when your school was closed because of the weather.

    Remember to include your **thoughts and feelings**.

    OR

12. **Write a short story** using the following opening:

    One by one, slowly, the children began to gather in the snow-filled park . . .

    You should develop **setting** and **character** as well as **plot**.

    OR

13. Winter is the best season of all.

    Give your views.

    OR

14. **Write in any way you choose** using the picture opposite as your inspiration.

[Turn over

FIRST   **Look at the picture opposite.
It shows a biker performing a stunt.**

NEXT   Think about sports and pastimes.

> WHAT YOU HAVE TO WRITE

15. **Write an informative article** for a magazine about an interesting sport or pastime.

    OR

16. **Write a short story** using the following title:

    No Fear

    You should develop **setting** and **character** as well as **plot**.

    OR

17. **Write about** an occasion when **preparing** for a competition was as important as the competition itself.

    Remember to include your **thoughts and feelings**.

    OR

18. It's just not worth it.

    Extreme sports are simply too risky.

    Give your views.

[Turn over for assignments 19 to 23 on *Page twelve*

There are no pictures for these assignments.

19. **Describe the scene** brought to mind by **ONE** of the following:

    On the tall peaks the glistening sunbeams play,
    With a light heart our course we may renew,
    The first whose footsteps print the mountain dew.

    OR

    In flakes of light upon the mountain side;
    Where with loud voice the power of water shakes
    The leafy wood, or sleeps in quiet lakes.

    William Wordsworth

    OR

20. We are all different, so we all learn differently.

    There are now lots of opportunities to learn in ways suited to the individual.

    Give your views.

    OR

21. My Dream Destination.

    Write about the one place in the world you would really like to visit.

    OR

22. We are a society motivated by money.

    Give your views.

    OR

23. **Write a short story** using the following title:

    The High Life

    You should develop **setting** and **character** as well as **plot**.

    [END OF QUESTION PAPER]

[BLANK PAGE]

Acknowledgements

Permission has been sought from all relevant copyright holders and Bright Red Publishing is grateful for the use of the following:

The article 'Saddle the white horses' by Dave Flanagan, taken from The Herald magazine 22 April 2006 © David Flanagan (2008 General Close Reading page 2);

An extract from 'Atonement' by Ian McEwan, published by Jonathan Cape. Reprinted by permission of The Random House Group (2008 Credit Close Reading pages 2 & 3);

A photograph taken from www.bigfoto.com (2008 F/G/C Writing page 2);

The photograph 'Chips are down' by Robert Perry taken from Scotland on Sunday, 2 July 2006 © The Scotsman Publications Ltd (2008 F/G/C Writing page 4);

The photograph 'Eye Opener' © Steve Double (2008 F/G/C Writing page 6);

The photograph 'Language Lesson' © Julie Brook (2008 F/G/C Writing page 8);

The photograph 'Airbus 320' by Ian Britton. Reproduced with permission of Freefoto.com (2008 F/G/C Writing page 10);

An extract from 'Labyrinth' by Kate Mosse, published by Orion Books, an imprint of the Orion Publishing Group, London (2009 General Close Reading pages 2 & 3);

An extract from 'When We Were Orphans' by Kazuo Ishiguro, published by Faber and Faber (2009 Credit Close Reading pages 2 & 3);

A photograph taken from www.bigfoto.com (2009 F/G/C Writing page 2);

A photograph © FRANCK FIFE/AFP/Getty Images (2009 F/G/C Writing page 4);

A photograph by Phil Wilkinson © The Scotsman Publications Ltd (2009 F/G/C Writing page 4);

The photograph 'Surfing. Saltburn by the Sea, Yorkshire' by Ian Britton. Reproduced with permission of Freefoto.com (2009 F/G/C Writing page 4);

A photograph of a girl ski-ing © Neil McQuoid (2009 F/G/C Writing page 4);

A photograph © Blackout Concepts/Alamy (2009 F/G/C Writing page 8);

The photograph 'I will survive: Learning to make fire without matches is a basic bushcraft skill © Roger Bamber/Alamy (2009 F/G/C Writing page 10);

The article 'Chimps Go Ape In Zoo' by Adam Forrest, taken from 'The Big Issue' Magazine, May 1–7 2008 © The Big Issue (2010 General Close Reading page 2);

'In the Silence' from The Black Halo by Iain Crichton Smith is reproduced by permission of Polygon, an imprint of Birlinn Ltd. www.birlinn.co.uk (2010 Credit Close Reading pages 2 & 3);

The photograph 'Pensioner with a skateboarding expert' © Newsquest (Herald & Times). Licensor www.scran.ac.uk (2010 F/G/C Writing page 2);

The photograph 'A street artist and his chalk drawing' © Marius Alexander. Licensor www.scran.ac.uk (2010 F/G/C Writing page 4);

The photograph 'Big Wheel' © Newsquest (Herald & Times). Licensor www.scran.ac.uk (2010 F/G/C Writing page 6);

A photograph © George Clerk/iStockphoto (2010 F/G/C Writing page 8);

The photograph 'Exterior of the Scottish Parliament Holyrood Building by night' © Scottish Parliament. Licensor www.scran.ac.uk (2010 F/G/C Writing page 8);

The photograph 'The aqueduct and boat lift, Falkirk Wheel, 2002' © Falkirk Museums. Licensor www.scran.ac.uk (2010 F/G/C Writing page 8);

The photograph 'Autumn ground shot with strewn leaves and long shadows' © Jack Stevenson. Licensor www.scran.ac.uk (2010 F/G/C Writing page 10);

The article 'Bright Lights Big City' by Janice Galloway, taken from The Sunday Herald Magazine, 2008 © Janice Galloway (2011 General Reading pages 2 & 3);

Two photographs © Herald & Times Group (2011 General Reading page 2);

The article 'Bouncing Off Walls' by Kenneth Stephen, taken from The Herald Magazine, 25/04/09 © Herald & Times Group (2011 Credit Reading page 2);

A photograph © Sergiy Goruppa/iStockphoto (2011 Credit Reading page 2);

A photograph © Martin Lee/Rex Images (2011 F/G/C Writing page 2);

A photograph © Adam Lau (2011 F/G/C Writing page 4);

A photograph © Catherine Yeulet/iStockphoto (2011 F/G/C Writing page 6);

A photograph © Daniel Yee (2011 F/G/C Writing page 8);

An article and two photographs by Kevin Rushby, taken from the travel section of 'Saturday Guardian' 23 January 2010. Copyright Guardian News & Media Ltd 2010 (2012 General Reading page 2);

An extract from 'Blink' by Malcolm Gladwell (Allen Lane, 2005). Copyright © Malcolm Gladwell, 2005. Reproduced by permission of Penguin Books Ltd (2012 Credit Reading pages 2 to 4);

Photograph of Balgownie Mill, Eassie, By Glamis. Presently owned by Mr C Heath, image © Bell Ingram Design, who are converting the existing mill into a dwelling house (2012 F/G/C Writing page 4);

Image taken from www.bigfoto.com (2012 F/G/C Writing page 8).

SQA STANDARD GRADE
GENERAL AND CREDIT ENGLISH 2008–2012

ENGLISH GENERAL
READING 2008

1. (a) (surfing) stickers

   (b) *Any two from*:
   - Thurso 23 miles away
   - have taken the right turn-off (for Thurso)
   - nearly at their destination

2. Short paragraph/one sentence paragraph
   OR reference to word choice "big league" suggests dramatic or similar

3. (a) Gloss of "tropical" eg hot/exotic/beach with palm trees

   (b) "raw"/"exposed"/"worst excesses of the Scottish climate"

4. The best (of all the Caithness surfing spots)

5. Reference to speed/power/ferocity/frightening/danger/(rolling) movement/size/shape
   (*Any two*)

6. (i) (first time) held in Scotland

   (ii) Furthest north it has been held

7. WCT gloss of "premier division" eg best competitors/higher status
   WQS gloss of "platform … to move up into the big time" eg step towards the better competition accept reference to lower status

8. (i) Reference to prize money

   (ii) (vital tour) points

9. (i) (enjoy) travelling/new place/adventure/new experience

   (ii) One of the best waves in Europe/big reef break waves

   (iii) Reference to photographs (*any three*)

10. Cold/harsh conditions

    OR reference to "Thurso is one of the best waves in Europe, if not the world."

11. Big/dramatic/exciting waves
    OR reference to challenging weather conditions OR reference to contrast with tropical events

12. They don't want/to protect from/to stop (or similar) overcrowding (or similar)

13. Informal/chatty/slang or similar

14. (i) Met surfers/addressed their concerns

    (ii) Paid for car park improvements

15. "most of them are positive" must have whole expression

16. boycott

17. (a)

very negative and angry	
quite pleased but worried	
excited and not really anxious	✓

   (b) *Any one from:*
   - "eagerly anticipating"

- "makes me feel proud"
- "don't think it's going to be that bad"
- "doesn't anticipate a negative impact"
- "it'll generate business for us"

18. (Thurso is) far away/unknown/like another world

19. (a) Negative: gloss of "live out of your bag a lot" eg few comforts/few belongings with you/never in one place for long/gloss of "long stints away from home" eg not at home for long periods of time

    (b) Positive: reference to seeing many/varied/new places OR gloss of "perform well" eg (competition) success OR gloss of "get some really good waves" eg good conditions/exciting surf/waves just right

20. (i) Length of ride

    (ii) Difficulty of moves

    (iii) How they connect it all together

21. (i)

to tell the reader some amusing stories about surfing	
to inform the reader about a surfing competition in Scotland	✓
to argue against holding a surfing competition in Scotland	

    (ii) Accept appropriate reference to information in the passage eg
    - surfing/the life of a surfer/the competition scoring system
    - Thurso as a surfing location/the WQS and WCT

ENGLISH CREDIT
READING 2008

1. Writing a play/organising or preparing for performance (of play)

2. (a) *Sentence structure:*
    list (of things she has done)/repetition (of verb structure)/parenthesis (to include extra tasks)/long sentence emphasises multiple nature of tasks

    (b) *Word choice:*
    (two-day) tempest (of composition) suggests energetic/feverish/dedicated approach

3. Relationship based on uncontrolled emotion/thoughtlessness or similar idea bound to end in disaster/misery/failure or similar idea

4. (a) (gently) mocking/ironic/thinks it's "over the top"/thinks it's unoriginal/thinks it's melodramatic less sophisticated answer eg it's not very good

    (b) Details: *Any one from:*
    *   "reckless passion"
    *   "Arabella"
    *   "wicked foreign count"
    *   "punished by ill fortune"
    *   "contracts cholera"
    *   "impetuous dash"
    *   "deserted by him and nearly everybody else"
    *   "bed-bound in an attic"
    *   "fortune presents her with a second chance"
    *   "impoverished doctor"
    *   "a prince in disguise"
    *   "work among the needy"
    *   "healed by him"
    *   "(rewarded by) reconciliation with her family"
    *   "wedding with the medical prince"
    *   "windy sunlit day in spring"

    Explanation:
    *   clichéd nature of plot/characters
    *   unlikely events
    *   over-dramatic
    *   like a fairy tale

5. She reacts as she thinks Briony wants her to/she is making an effort to respond in appropriate way Suggestion of insincerity also accepted

6. *Any two from:*
    *   Briony's arm round mother's shoulder
    *   mother takes Briony in her arms/onto her lap
    *   mother whispering in Briony's ear
    *   Briony watching mother's face carefully for reaction
    *   Briony values mother's opinion
    *   mother wants to please Briony by her reaction
    *   Briony plans to put mother's opinion on poster.

7. "(made her) heart thud" suggests excitement
    OR "luminous" suggests brilliant, vivid quality
    OR "yearning" suggests deep longing

8. Reference to positive reaction eg moved/involved/proud/admiring/thrilled supported by any suitable quotation eg "buckled in grief"/ "boasting"/"my younger sister, Briony Tallis the writer"/"you must surely have heard of her"/"punched the air"/ "exultation"/"provoke his admiration"

9. *Any two from:*
    *   gloss of "celebrate his return" eg make his homecoming special
    *   gloss of "provoke his admiration" eg make him proud
    *   gloss of "guide him ... girlfriends" eg stop him having so many relationships
    *   gloss of "the right form of wife" eg find suitable wife

10. (a) Briony: organised/obsessive or similar sister: messy/ lackadaisical or similar

    (b) (i) *Sentence structure:*
        sister: list/repetition and suitable comment
        Briony: list/parenthesis/colon and suitable comment
        Reference to 'Whereas' introducing idea of contrast also acceptable.

        (ii) *Word choice:*
        sister:
        *   "stew (of unclosed ...)"
        *   "unclosed books"
        *   "unfolded clothes"
        *   "unmade bed"
        *   "unemptied ashtrays"
            suggests relaxed/untidy/muddled approach
        Briony:
        *   "shrine"
        *   "controlling demon"
        *   "all facing one way"
        *   "toward their owner"
        *   "neatly corralled"
        *   "only tidy"
        *   "straight-backed"
        *   "under strict instructions"
        *   "even ranks and spacing"
        *   "citizen army"
        *   "(awaiting) orders"
            suggests her (need for) tidiness/abnormal organisation

11. Parenthesis/adding extra information about how controlling she is

12. *Reference to any two from*:
    *   secret drawer
    *   locked diary
    *   code/safe/secret numbers/floorboard

13. Indicates/introduces list of things she has been collecting

14. Varied interests/imaginative/interested in the strange or magical or macabre or beautiful or world of nature

15. (i) Gloss of "foolish" eg silly

    (ii) *Any two from:*
    *   gloss of "imitative" eg like other stories
    *   gloss of "lacking ... world" eg no wisdom about/experience of the world
    *   gloss of "clumsy" eg unsophisticated

16. People would think it was about Briony herself

17. Immune

18. (normally) shy/reserved or similar, (very) confident or similar

19. Beautiful: not much to say/all the same
    Ugly: endless possibilities/more interesting (because different)

20. (i) Imaginative: reference to appropriate evidence eg
    *   "two-day tempest of composition"
    *   "little playlets in themselves"
    *   "imagination itself was a source of secrets"
    *   makes up stories
        and appropriate explanation
        OR any two appropriate references

(ii) Anxious: reference to appropriate evidence eg
- "made her wince"
- "too vulnerable"
- "too embarrassing"
- excessive tidiness
  and appropriate explanation
  OR any two appropriate references

ENGLISH GENERAL READING 2009

1. (historical) dig/archaeology

2. danger/problem/difficulty
   linked to job

3. *Any three from:*
   Alice is thirsty/drink is warmed up
   heat haze/blue sky

4. (*a*) list (of activities)

   (*b*) "digging"/"scraping"/"cataloguing"/
   "recording"/(use of) verbs

5. "demoralised"/"little to justify their efforts"/"only a few
   fragments"/"couple of arrowheads"

6. *Any two from:*
   tired/sore legs/sore shoulders/reference to lack of
   success/reference to colleagues taking a break

7.

She wants to show that she can do the job herself	True
She does not like her colleagues	Cannot tell
She wants to share her discovery	False

8. (*a*) "(flutter of) excitement"

   (*b*) "(knows) she's got something worth finding"/"telling
   herself not to expect too much"

9. to emphasise care/slowness

10. absorbed

11. *Any two from:*
    "so absorbed"/"doesn't notice"/"world seems to hang
    suspended"/"mesmerised"

12. big OR heavy stone not (normally) graceful

13. reference to alliteration

14. realises (gloss of "it sinks in") she nearly died or "how very
    close she came to being crushed" (gloss of "how very close she
    came to being crushed")

15. reference to opening in mountain
    distracts her/curiosity/drawn towards it/wants to keep it to
    herself

16. *Any two from:*
    big/strong/prevents people going in the entrance//keeps cave
    and contents safe/reference to personification

17. reference to "(velvet) black" becoming "(charcoal) grey"
    reference to sees tunnel/can see what lies ahead

18. (i) anxious/scared

    (ii) feels she is doing something wrong

19. *Any two from:*
    short/paragraph on its own/reference to "abruptly" eg sudden
    change in her feelings/cliffhanger OR
    makes reader want to know what happened next

20. makes you feel it is happening now/feel you're there as it's
    happening/makes you feel involved

21. (i) if 'return to colleagues' accept references to growing
    feelings that she should seek help/her injuries/frightening
    situation/desire to show colleagues the buckle

    (ii) if 'go further in' accept references to something drawing

her in/excited about buckle/adventurous/
determined/independent/
if 'trapped' accept references to something drawing her
in/unease at end/eeriness of cave/falling stone

ENGLISH CREDIT READING 2009

1. (a) Uncle Philip with mother so mother safe

   (b) anxious/not relaxed

2. "For the first time in weeks"

3. generous: plans to bu

y gift for Christopher

   caring: wants to make Christopher happy by treating
              him/has seen piano accordion in window and
              thought of Christopher/eager to buy it before
              someone else does OR to avoid disappointment

4. *Any three from:*

   rushed downstairs/jumped last (four) steps/circled
   adults/reference to flapped arms OR pretended to be bird of
   prey

5. *Any two from:*

   reference to she has not laughed like this for some time/end of
   anxious time/return to normality/pleased at mother's
   happiness

6. parenthesis/gives extra information about the
   atmosphere/Christopher's feelings OR situation

7. be less or not alert for danger/be (more) trusting/be less or no
   longer worried (about his mother)

8. (i) might not be allowed to go/might change mind (about
       accordion)

   (ii) might ruin (happy) mood

9. *Any two from:*

   reference to grasped Christopher's shoulder/use of commands
   OR

   exclamation marks/tells Christopher to wave again

10. trouble to come/realises later this was significant/realises he
    was being naïve

11. usual behaviour while travelling

12. (wide) streets with trees OR greenery

    small/busy streets/reference to driver shouting to get
    pedestrians and traffic out of the way

13. plans to abandon him/delay his return

14. (i) "clogged (with people)"

    (ii) "(good-humoured) throng"

    (iii) "jostling (crowd)"

15. effective comment on significance of light eg
    security/openness/safety

    effective comment on significance of darkness eg
    mystery/deceit/threat reference to change of mood/turning
    point

16. (a) *Any two from:*

    "(feeling rising from) the pit of my stomach"/"(great)
    horror"/"saw in my face that the game was up"

    (b) *Any two from:*

    "terrible confusion"/"trembling with emotion"/"grasped
    my shoulder"

17. trying to justify himself/trying to get through to
    Christopher/trying to avoid being blamed by
    Christopher/making Christopher remember these words

18. (*a*) "forced"/"pushing"/"violently"/"squeezing"/
"abandoning" indicating his desperation/urgency/
difficulty

OR "people laughed"/"called angrily" suggests
indifference of those around him to his misery

OR "confused"/"trying to form in my head" suggest
uncertainty

(*b*) reference to long sentence/many phrases (punctuated by
commas) suggests long journey home/struggle

OR repetition of "sometimes" (with verb) suggests
difficulty of getting through crowds

OR short sentence at end of paragraph suggests dramatic
climax

19. proper behaviour

20. panting/exhaustion/reference to "little more than walking
pace"
"did not stop at all"

21. emphasises certainty of disaster/terrible reality (hitting
Christopher)/suggests Christopher's anticipation/evokes
sympathy for Christopher

22. Explanation   suitable reason for her disappearance eg
abduction/murder/plan in which Uncle Philip
was involved

Evidence   possible answers include Christopher's ongoing
anxiety before event/mother seems happy (and
unsuspecting)/Christopher's haunting final view of
mother/reference to Uncle Philip's behaviour

ENGLISH GENERAL READING 2010

1. *Any two from:*
outside/on the other side of the glass from chimp enclosure at
the zoo

2. *Any two from:*
(i) eating boiled egg/
(ii) travelling in ship/reference to "snooty gesture"

3. *Any two from:*
reference to stops what he is doing/reference to change in facial
expression/reference to goes back to eating

4. *Any three from:*
(i) enclosure "state-of-the-art"/"air-conditioned"/ "cost 5.6
million pounds"/
(ii) "luxury"/"largest chimp enclosure in the world"/
(iii) "higher standard of living than most humans"

5. active: "longest"
or "(most) intricate climbing frame"
safe: moat

6. ordinary/house   (millionaire's) mansion

7. they can study the chimps
in environment similar to the wild

8. Proud   gloss of "he helped design" enclosure eg involved
in planning
Delighted   gloss of "realised so spectacularly" eg worked out
so well/dream came true
or reference to public reaction

9. *Any two from:*
"(cartoon) game"/"children learn chimp gestures"/
"kids will be running around, touching everything"

10.

Rather uninterested	
Very enthusiastic	✓
Slightly critical	

He was model for cartoon game/he demonstrates chimp
movements for writer/reference to "as they should"

11. Link with conservation work/research into threats to chimps in
the Budongo Forest/Uganda

12. Gloss of "habitat destruction" eg homes disappearing
Gloss of "traps set for bush meat" eg hunted for food

13.

To study closely	
To help	
To relate to	
To tell apart	✓

14. (*a*) "personalities"/reference to personality traits
"(glossy monthly) magazine"
(*b*) to get people interested in them/to identify with them/to
attract visitors

15. alliteration

16. he could become leader
too young/thin (just now)/still learning things

17. (*a*) eating on his own/mixing with humans/reference to lack of
interaction with other chimps
(*b*) reference to grooming (a bit more)

18. (i) reference to size/height of enclosure
(ii) reference to soil

(iii) reference to behaviour

19. their language varies
in different places

20. gloss of "fresh marvels" eg new discoveries or similar
gloss of "daily basis" eg every day/regularly/always or similar

21. reference to watching chimps eg "noting the quirks of the
Budongo 11"
reference to communicating with chimps eg "say hello"

22. (i) appropriate for/sums up subject matter
(ii) "go ape" suggests extreme behaviour

23.

To argue that animals like chimps should not be kept in zoos	
To give a positive, informative view of the new enclosure	✓
To request donations for the upkeep of the new enclosure	

reference to positive feature of enclosure eg
comfort/activities/size/link to conservation work

ENGLISH CREDIT READING 2010

1. Playing (hide and seek)
with friends/in the fields/at night

2. (face and hands) sweaty/(knees) trembling
+ suitable explanation

3. "(Their voices were) like bells in the distance"
Echoing/fading/musical/in sequence/carrying (over the fields)

4. (a) Climax of first part of story/beginning of the "real"
story/the moment he realises the others have gone/suggests
his isolation
(b) short sentence/end of paragraph

5. people

6. (a) metaphor
(b) *Any two from:*
straight/long
or stretches into the distance/(almost) "solid"
quality/bright/contrasts with darkness

7. parenthesis/adding more information/giving examples
about the types of creatures (which might have been there)

8. treasure chests
dead bodies (on a battlefield)

9. *Any two from:*
gloss of "continually distracted by shadows" eg put off by
dark/gloss of "not at all good at arithmetic" eg not skilled in
counting/gloss of "more imaginative than mathematical" eg
more creative/gloss of "only seven" eg quite young

10. Repetition of "twelve"
short sentences

11. beautiful   reference to "jewels"
menacing   reference to cold eyes/killing of mouse

12. reference to (growing) darkness
reference to silence

13. (he is) the only person there (so feels responsible)

14. "forbidding"/"(my) kingdom"/"you are not to do"/"I don't wish
you to do"/"commanded" and suitable explanation eg night as a
ruler/night making demands **or** threats

15. reference to stooks dancing/ "unreal"/ "ghostly"/boys "gone to
another country"/ "pulling the roofs over their heads"

16. noisy v. quiet
or brightness (eg sun, red) v. darkness
or active v. still

17. repetition of "strawy"/"sharp" **or** list: "deep and rough and
sharp"
or contrast: "not at all ... thorns"
or simile: "like the voice of stones, thorns"
or onomatopoeia: eg "(busy and) hissing"/ "whispering"
or alliteration: "strawy voices ... strawy language"
or word choice eg "deep", "rough", "sharp", "whispering" and
suitable explanation

18. *Any two from:*
reference to "came closer together"/"pressed against each
other"/"thorny"
or "spiky (wall)"/"screamed"/extra stook/unlucky
number/"heart beating irregularly"

19. mirrors Iain's thinking/creates suspense/involves reader

20. (a) "moving towards him"/"sharp teeth"/"thorny

fingers"/"sighing"/
reference to old man **or** old woman/"(sigh was)
despairing" and suitable comment

   (b) "sighing"/"straw peeling away from them"/ "(finally) they
were no longer there"/"returned to their boxes"/"pulled
the roofs over their heads" and suitable comment

21. reference to approaching the stook/comfort/sleep/ security
v.
thorns/thirteenth/fear/nightmare quality of previous paragraph

22. imaginative   reference to appropriate evidence
eg scout/pirate/thirteenth stook/stooks were
talking/stooks were moving/boys appearing next
day/night as a powerful figure

    young   reference to appropriate evidence eg hide and
seek/excited during the game/aged seven/never
been out so late/scared of the stooks

ENGLISH GENERAL READING 2011

1. special link with Christmas/identified Glasgow with Christmas/
when she thought of Glasgow she thought of Christmas/
important event/or similar idea

2. lived at seaside   did not swim
OR appreciated beauty   broke ornaments

3. alliteration/list

4. *Any three from:*
dazzle/warmth of crowds/(snowy) shop displays/cheer/
hundreds of trees/lights

5. Did   "rolling her eyes"
Said   "Our town is a dump"/"(We've only a) daft wee tree"

6. *Any two from:*
ref to made to dress up/mother cleaning her face with spit or
hurting her face/warning her about gloves

7. paragraph on its own/sentence on its own/short sentence

8. could see very little (ref to "our view was strips"/"visible in
glimpses") due to dirty windows (ref to "filthy"/"through
grime")

9. *Any two from:*
"big enough for trains to roll right inside"/"high as
cliffs"/"pigeons indoors"/"clock the size of our bathroom"
lift or gloss acceptable

10. *Any two from:*
(a) metaphor/simile/alliteration/assonance
(b) flying up/flying away/taking off/spreading their wings

11. *Any two from:*
"(buildings coated in velvet-deep) soot"/"charcoal-coloured
(statues)"/"ash-grey (walls)"/general comment on dirty or dark
features

12. "my face brushing against the tweedy coats of strangers"

13. parenthesis/extra information
to show writer does not agree/it is mother's opinion

14. beard lop-sided/at an angle (gloss of "squinty")
elastic too long/does not fit (gloss of "elastic…stretched too
far")

15. *Any two from:*
shoved her/lifted her up/placed her (on his knee)

16. *Any two from:*
"(miniature) butcher's tools"/ "whatever they were for"/"(little
pink) cutlery set"

17. *Any two from:*
ref to uncertainty ("Whatever they were for")/positive reaction
("lovely")/could not believe she was allowed to keep it ("It
took…mine")

18. high up/looking down/above the lights and bells

19. nothing was bought (apart from food)/they had come for the
lights (not to buy things)

20. *Any two from:*
ref to "natural"/number/movement/sound

21. *Any two from:*
mother had to pull her away/ref to "All the way back"/sister was
right or would not have imagined it/ref to magic

22. gloves were dirty
experience of the birds

23. (still) feeds birds at Christmas
first thing

24. If "Yes" suitable ref eg words or actions of sister or mother/
child's reaction to train journey or station or store or Santa or
birds
If "No" suitable ref eg unlikely small child more excited by
birds than Christmas toys/Santa

ENGLISH CREDIT
READING 2011

1. sets the scene/creates immediacy/highlights everyday nature of
scene/involves reader

2. "bound (over rocks)"/"sure-footed"/"leaping"/"like
cats"/"trainers crunching into the gravel"/"roll on to their
shoulders"/"springing (up)"/"pushing off"/"fluid"/"unbroken"/
"up and over a wall"/"vaulting (a railing)" plus suitable
comment eg suggests speed/energy/flexibility

3. gloss of "unorthodox" eg different/alternative
gloss of "urban theatre" eg drama/show based in a city/street

4. ref to freedom eg go where you choose
ref to speed
gloss of "interesting"

5. metaphor
suggests winding/curved

6. list from "bollards" to "high walls" or of things more difficult
to climb
OR ref to climax "whole buildings"

7. *Any two from:*
gloss of "dynamic images" eg exciting pictures/gloss of "lured
youngsters out" eg encouraged young people to go outdoors/
ref. to change from passivity to activity

8. (*a*) *Any two from:*
featured in films/used by clothing firms/ref to different
cities
(*b*) *Any two from:*
trendy/underground/different/not 'safe'/breaks rules/
spontaneous/or similar ideas

9. "Therein" refers back to previous paragraph (why it is popular)
"the problem" refers forward to paragraph 8 (explanation of
why popularity has created problems)/sensible comment on
"though"

10. cause/reason/contributory factor/accelerant

11. gloss of "dangerous jumps (across tenements)"/"flips and
tricks"/commercialism versus
gloss of "fine-tuning the mind and body"/"overcome obstacles
and fear"/individual pursuit

12. (*a*) got more people involved/raised awareness (gloss of
"popularised")
(*b*) caused misunderstanding (gloss of "responsible for a lot of
misconceptions")

13. fuller understanding/wider acceptance of parkour
encourage people to come and watch

14.

Concerned, in case they injure themselves	
Jealous, because they are so talented	
Admiring, because they show skill and care	✓
Dismissive, because it is a worthless activity	

15. help fight obesity
encourage risk-taking

16. adult: "more than 100"/many people attend
schools: schools "have requested further sessions"

17. *Any two from:*
"innocuous" means harmless
but the injury happened at the posts
ref to irony

18. simile
suggests balance/skill/grace/high up/hint of danger/like performer or similar idea

19. Meaning   official procedures/paperwork or similar idea
Context   liability insurance/(signed) disclaimers/risk assessment

20. *Any two from:*
ref to male and female/students/teachers/age
more general comment eg different sorts of people

21. shows that women also involved/professional/educated/older/ from Munich: international element/positive role model/ref to positive content of interview

22. measuring dangers (gloss of "It makes any risk…go")/make yourself achieve more (gloss of "pushing…time")/work out difficulties (gloss of "assess problems")/approach life with strength (gloss of "take…life")

23. *Any two suitable supporting explanations from:*
If "Pushing yourself…" refs to eg mental fitness/ physical fitness/agility/Angie Rupp's views/Chris Grant's training or coaching
If "Allowing anyone to achieve…" refs to eg variety of people taking part/impact on everyday life
If "Being an individual…" refs to eg (unfair) criticism by media/Glynn Forsythe's views/Paragraph 4 "individuals find their own way"

ENGLISH GENERAL READING 2012

1. walking them/tiring them out/ref. to conversations with people (lifts acceptable)

2. gloss of 'want proper walks' eg need more exercise
gloss of 'want sticks thrown' eg need to be entertained

3. informal/chatty/colloquial etc

4. *Any two from:*
ref. to friendly/good-natured/calm/lying down
or asleep/unobtrusive/no trouble

5. *Any three from:*
runs riot/eats crisps people have dropped
sneaks into a neighbour's room/sniffs luggage (for food)
(lift or gloss acceptable)

6. No ✔
('they) laugh'/'(You're a) lovable (chap)'

7. Wilf   sleeps soundly
Owner   difficulty sleeping/disturbed sleep/anxious

8. ref. to limited daylight

9. ref. to stock-training
ref. to Wilf's being small
(lift or gloss acceptable)

10. 'bounding'/'(as if he's) on springs'
appropriate explanation eg full of energy/happy/excited/ appropriate ref. to movement

11. *Any three from:*
beautiful (building)/location/kitchen equipment
foam mattresses/well swept
(lift or gloss acceptable)

12. shop is closed
'breakfast and lunch will finish food supplies'
(lift or gloss acceptable)

13. 'old slate-mine workings'/'industrial history
V. 'wind farms'

14. gloss of 'tired but happy' eg contented/looking forward (to meal)
gloss of 'hopes are dashed' eg disappointment

15. *Any two from:*
basic kitchen/(black) plastic on mattresses/
no heating (lift or gloss acceptable)

16. (*a*) it is dog food/Wilf will not share
(*b*) ref. to phone difficulty
ref. to expense of taxi

17. alliteration

18. *Any three from:*
clouds/sunlight
snow/whiteout
(lift or gloss acceptable)

19. Word choice   'horror'
Sentence structure   parenthesis/short sentence
Climax

20. Cautious ✔

21. *Any two from:*
'rising wind'/ **or** 'cold wind'/'driving snow into our faces' **or** 'icy snow' or 'snow into our faces'/rerouting
'bridge being washed away'

22. proud/feeling positive
    ref to 'He was a breed'/comments of passer by

23. Candidates may approach this question in one of two ways ie,
    they may separate the achievements of family and Wilf (in
    which case an example must be given) **or** treat them as a shared
    experience. In either case ref. should be made to any two of
    challenges/rite of passage/distance/height/fell terriers

24. To describe the challenges they faced on their trip. ✔
    ref to appropriate evidence eg Weather/anecdotes about Wilf/
    difficulties encountered/miles covered

ENGLISH CREDIT READING 2012

1. Sell the statue to them/trick them

2. Doubt

3. (a) '(badly) damaged'/'(in) fragments'
      '(almost) perfectly preserved'
   (b) *Any two from:*
      only about two hundred in existence/light-coloured glow/
      close to seven feet tall

4. took on loan **or** did not buy Kouros immediately/
   began thorough investigation/ref. to questions
   asked/involvement of legal dept
   (lift or gloss acceptable)

5. *Any two from:*
   spent two days examining surface/removed core
   sample/analysed sample/ref. to number of pieces of equipment/
   ref. to nature of equipment eg high-tech, sophisticated,
   advanced
   (lift or gloss acceptable)

6. ref. to extremely long time taken for calcite to form
   suggests age of statue/suggests statue was genuine

7. (shows) importance of find/(shows) wide interest in find

8. 'However (the kouros)' suggests change of direction (from
   acceptance in Paragraph 4)
   'problem' introduces the idea (that statue was not 'right'), to be
   developed in Paragraph 5

9. put into words   straight away

10. ('instinctive) sense that something was amiss'

11. (a) onomatopoeia
    (b) Proudly/dramatically/theatrically
        Less sophisticated answer eg quickly

12. An old statue does not **or** should not suggest something new

13. he had been involved in digs uncovering Kouros fragments
    ref. to difference in appearance eg fragments did not look clean,
    new etc, statue did not look as if it had been buried

14. immediacy/makes reader feel as if witness to the exchange **or**
    drama eg shock value/unexpected bluntness of Hoving's
    comments

15. Meaning: meeting conference (involving experts)
    Context: ref. to 'sculpture experts'/'chorus of dismay'/
    'consensus among…attendees'/'world's foremost experts'

16. ('wave') suggests overwhelming/sudden (feeling)

17. Careful/over long time/scientific
    Instinctive/sudden

18. Parenthesis/adding extra information
    how short a time it took to emphasise

19. (i) and (ii)   The four techniques are:
                 question + answer/short sentences/repitition/italics
                 Explanation should show awareness of emphasis/
                 drama/inexplicable knowledge/certainty

20. sudden decisions/first impressions/ref. to example(s) in first
    sentence of paragraph 14

21. decreasing numbers of seconds
    (Indicate) how short a time is needed to form (accurate)
    judgement

22. first impressions same as those formed over long period of time

23. Identification of appropriate feature eg Short/use of questions/direct address to reader/ref. to 'two seconds' **or** identification of relationship between paragraph and topic of passage/paragraph sums of passage plus appropriate comment

ENGLISH WRITING—2008 TO 2012

	Credit	*General*	*Foundation*
As the task requires. The candidate can	The work displays some distinction in ideas, construction and language. This is shown by a detailed attention to the purposes of the writing task; by qualities such as knowledge, insight, imagination; and by development that is sustained. Vocabulary, paragraphing and sentence construction are accurate and varied.	The work shows a general awareness of the purposes of the writing task. It has a number of appropriate ideas and evidence of structure. Vocabulary is on the whole accurate, but lacks variety.	The work shows a few signs of appropriateness and commitment to the purposes of the writing task.
	convey information, selecting and highlighting what is most significant;	convey information in some kind of sequence;	convey simple information;
	marshall ideas and evidence in support of an argument; these ideas have depth and some complexity; he/she is capable of objectivity, generalisation and evaluation;	order and present ideas and opinions with an attempt at reasoning;	present ideas and opinions in concrete personal terms;
	give a succinct account of a personal experience: the writing has insight and self-awareness;	give a reasonably clear account of a personal experience with some sense of involvement;	convey the gist of a personal experience;
	express personal feelings and reactions sensitively;	express personal feelings and reactions with some attempt to go beyond bald statement;	make a bald statement of personal feelings or reactions;
	display some skills in using the conventions of a chosen literary form, and in manipulating language to achieve particular effects.	use some of the more obvious conventions of a chosen literary form, and occasionally use language to achieve particular effects.	display a rudimentary awareness of the more obvious conventions of a chosen literary form, and occasionally attempt to use language to achieve particular effects.

A combination of these qualities may be called for by any one writing task.

| Intelligibility and Correctness | Writing which the candidate submits as finished work communicates meaning clearly at a first reading. Sentence construction is accurate and formal errors will not be significant. | Writing which the candidate submits as finished work communicates meaning at first reading. There are some lapses in punctuation, spelling and sentence construction. | Writing which the candidate submits as finished work communicates meaning largely at first reading: however, some further reading is necessary because of obtrusive formal errors and/or structural weaknesses, including inaccurate sentence construction and poor vocabulary. |

Length	When it is appropriate to do so, the candidate can sustain the quality of writing at some length. Pieces of extended writing submitted in the folio of coursework should not normally exceed 800 words in length. The overriding consideration is, however, that the length should be appropriate to the purposes of the writing task.		Length is appropriate to the purposes of the writing task.		100 words is to be taken as a rough guide to the minimum length expected for each finished piece of work, but the overriding consideration should be that the length is appropriate to the purposes of the writing task.	
	Grade 1	*Grade 2*	*Grade 3*	*Grade 4*	*Grade 5*	*Grade 6*
Differentiating Factors	The finished communication is not only clear; it is also stylish. Attention to purpose is not only detailed; it is also sensitive. Writing shows overall distinction in ideas, construction and language. Vocabulary is apt and extensive, and paragraphing and sentence construction are skilful. In these respects performance transcends the level of accuracy and variety acceptable at grade 2.	Evidence of one or more of the qualities of distinction in ideas, construction or language is present but these qualities are less well sustained and/or combined than at grade 1. In the main writing is substantial, accurate and relevant, but it lacks the insight, economy and style which characterises achievement at grade 1.	Writing is characterised by overall adequacy of communication. It conveys its meaning clearly and sentence construction and paragraphing are on the whole accurate. There is a reasonably sustained attention to purpose, and structure shows some coherence. Where appropriate there is a measure of generalisation and objectivity in reasoning.	Writing approaches the qualities of adequacy required for grade 3 but is clearly seen to be impaired in one of the following ways: there are significant inaccuracies in sentence construction. or the work is thin in appropriate ideas. or the work is weak in structure.	Writing rises a little above basic intelligibility and rudimentary attention to purpose. Formal errors and weaknesses are obtrusive but not as numerous as at grade 6. Attention to the purposes of the writing task is weak but the quality of the writer's ideas is perceptibly stronger than at grade 6.	Writing contains many formal errors and structural weaknesses but they do not overall have the effect of baffling the reader. The conveying of simple information is marked by obscurities and extraneous detail, and the presentation of ideas, opinions and personal experience is somewhat rambling and disjointed.

ENGLISH WRITING — 2008

Narrative Numbers 1, 7, 9, 12, 16, 20.

Task specifications/rubric/purposes

The criteria demand appropriate ideas and evidence of structure which in the narrative genre involve **plot** or **content** or **atmosphere**.

Note that the development of setting and character as well as plot is an explicit requirement for all of the short story options.

No 1 *Short story*: imposed opening should be continued.

No 7 *Short story*: imposed title **The School Gate** should be reflected in the narrative.

No 9 *Short story*: choice of imposed titles from which the candidates must select ONE from either **Seeing is Believing** or **Close Up**. Title selected must be reflected in the narrative.

No 12 *Short story*: imposed opening should be continued.

No 16 *Short story*: choice of imposed title from which candidates must select ONE from either **A New Beginning** or **Touchdown**. Title selected must be reflected in the narrative.

No 20 *Short story*: imposed opening should be continued.

Grade Differentiation

1 : 2 *Grade 1* narrative will show **overall distinction** in IDEAS, CONSTRUCTION and LANGUAGE, and will be both **stylish and skilful,** while *Grade 2* narrative will fall short both in the quality and in the **combination** of skills.

3 : 4 *Grade 3* responses will have an **appropriate plot,** will make use of appropriate **register** to create ATMOSPHERE or SUSPENSE and should include NARRATIVE or DESCRIPTIVE details to establish the main lines of the plot. Do not forget that lack of variety in plot and language skills is typical of *Grade 3*. Accuracy is the criterion to establish here.

Grade 4's **simple plot** will approach the adequacy of *Grade 3* but may be poorly organised or have significant inaccuracies.

5 : 6 *Grade 5*'s **very basic plot** will occasionally try to achieve particular effects, and it will also be poorly organised and have significant inaccuracies.

Grade 6 will have a combination of negative features, will be **rambling,** or have **obscurities** in the plot and the marker will have difficulty in decoding because of very poor spelling, sentencing, or handwriting.

NB If candidates ignore the rubric in respect of plot or character this may place them in *Grade 5* in terms of purpose ('few signs of appropriateness'), unless there are other strong compensating features ('accurate', 'varied', 'sensitive'). Where there are no strong compensating features, this may tip the balance overall into *Grade 6*.

Discursive/Informative Numbers 2, 5, 10, 13, 15, 18, 19, 21.

Task specifications/rubrics/purposes

The rubrics cover controversial issues which are likely to elicit emotional responses. Objectivity is not required but clear, straightforward presentation of a point of view is required. At all levels, candidates must deal with the specific topics or, as is the case in one of the tasks, use the imposed format to convey information about a specific activity.

No 2 *Agree/disagree or balanced view.* Candidates may choose to deal with the topic from one particular point of view or take a more balanced approach to the topic. Some background knowledge is required. Personal/anecdotal evidence may figure but should be used to support the candidate's argument.

No 5 *Agree/disagree/balanced view.* Personal or anecdotal evidence may very well feature but should follow a line of thought.

No 10 *Agree/disagree/balanced view.* Personal or anecdotal evidence may well feature but should pursue a line of thought.

No 13 *Agree/disagree/balanced.* Personal/anecdotal evidence may be present but this should pursue a line of thought.

No 15 *Agree/disagree/balanced view.* Some background knowledge is required. Personal/anecdotal evidence is likely to be used but it should reinforce the argument.

No 18 *Imposed format of informative article for school magazine.* The purpose here, however, is W1 to convey information. Some latitude may be required in terms of the degree/extent of the anecdotal/personal. This, too, may influence the tone but is acceptable as it is within the parameters of the rubric.

No 19 *Agree/disagree or balanced view.* Personal/anecdotal evidence is very likely to feature in responses to this rubric.

No 21 *Agree/disagree or balanced.* Both facets of education must be covered (inside and outside). A clear line of thought/argument should be presented with supporting evidence. Anecdotal evidence is, again, likely to feature but should be used to pursue a line of thought.

Grade Differentiation – Discursive

1 : 2 *Grade 1* responses will show a **combination of depth, complexity and skilful deployment** of ideas, and will also marshall evidence in support of an argument.

Grade 2 responses will lack this combination of technical skill and confident tone, presenting ideas in a **less developed** or **sustained** manner.

3 : 4 *Grade 3* will attempt an orderly flow of ideas, which may not succeed logically, whereas *Grade 4* will be typically **weak in structure,** or **have thin ideas** or poorly constructed sentences.

5 : 6 *Grade 5* will present ideas and opinions in **concrete, personal terms** which may be anecdotal, but are more than a bald series of unsupported, **disjointed** or **rambling** statements, the hallmarks of *Grade 6*.

Grade Differentiation – Informative

1 : 2 *Grade 1* will convey information in a **clear sequence, selecting and highlighting** what is most significant. *Grade 2* responses will be **less well sustained** in terms of the qualities of distinction in **ideas, construction and language.**

3 : 4 *Grade 3* will convey the relevant information **in some kind of sequence** which may not succeed logically, whereas *Grade 4* will be **weak in structure** or have **thin ideas** or **weak sentence construction.**

5 : 6 *Grade 5* will convey only **simple information.** Formal errors will be obtrusive but the writing will not be marked by the **rambling** and **disjointed** statements which define *Grade 6.*

Personal Experience/Descriptive Numbers 3, 4, 6, 8, 11, 22.

Task specifications/rubric/purposes

Each of the above calls for a personal response; while there are no genre requirements here, content must be specific and appropriate.

No 3 A single occasion is required. The idea of both the 'journey' and the 'unexpected' should be presented although some latitude should be allowed with the latter. Associated thoughts and feelings should be rendered.

No 4 Some latitude is required here. There may be some overlaps across W1 (conveying information) and W3 (conveying feelings and reactions) and possibly even W2 (deploying ideas).

No 6 The rubric restricts the candidate to a single occasion, although a number of scenes may be used to progress the idea of tested loyalty.

No 8 A single occasion is required. The nature of the 'authority' should be interpreted liberally. The evocation of both thoughts and feelings is an explicit requirement of the rubric.

No 11 A single occasion is required. The idea of the value of the lesson is clearly very open. The lesson, however, must be learned from 'an older relative.' Again, thoughts and feelings should be expressed.

No 22 Description of a scene is an explicit requirement of the rubric. Candidates should choose ONE of the two options.

Grade Differentiation

1 : 2 *Grade 1* will be a well crafted, stylish account and will deploy a range of skills to express perceptiveness and self-awareness and to achieve or create effects, while a *Grade 2* account will be soundly constructed and show a **measure of insight** and self-awareness expressed accurately. *Grade 2* may not be succinct but will be **substantial.**

3 : 4 A *Grade 3* response will be reasonably well sustained, with easily grasped structure, and will on the whole be correct but with a certain dull monotony.

Grade 4 will be structurally weak and thin in ideas but will still **attempt involvement, approaching the overall adequacy** of *Grade 3.*

5 : 6 *Grade 5* may have positive features such as a runaway enthusiasm which may detract the stated purpose but it will present the **gist** of the experience without **ramblings** and incoherence which, along with **numerous errors** and near-illegible handwriting are the mark of *Grade 6.*

Free Choice Numbers 14, 17.

Task specification/rubric/purposes

This question calls for the candidate to determine the purpose of the writing and format. It is, therefore, important that the candidate's writing purpose is made clear in the course of the response. Markers should assess according to the appropriate criteria.

No 14 The rubric restricts the candidate to the use of the picture and its associated ideas.

No 17 The rubric restricts the candidate to the use of the picture and its associated ideas.

ENGLISH WRITING—2009

Narrative Numbers: 3, 7, 11, 14, 16, 21.
Task specifications/rubric/purposes
The criteria demand appropriate ideas and evidence of structure which in the narrative genre involve **plot** or **content** or **atmosphere**.

Note that the development of setting and character as well as plot is an explicit requirement for all of the short story options.

No 3 short story - imposed opening should be continued. Candidates may choose to adopt the persona of the gargoyle and this is perfectly acceptable.

No 7 short story – imposed title **Against the Odds** must be reflected in the narrative.

No 11 short story – choice of imposed titles from which the candidates must select ONE from either **The Animal Kingdom** or **Animal Magic**. Title selected must be reflected in the narrative.

No 14 short story – imposed opening should be continued.

No 16 imposed title **Trapped in the Forest** must be reflected in the narrative.

No 21 imposed title **Paradise Lost** must be reflected in the narrative.

Grade Differentiation

1 : 2 Grade 1 narrative will show **overall distinction** in IDEAS, CONSTRUCTION and LANGUAGE, and will be both **stylish and skilful**, while Grade 2 narrative will fall short both in the quality and in the **combination** of skills.

3 : 4 Grade 3 responses will have an **appropriate plot**, will make use of appropriate **register** to create ATMOSPHERE or SUSPENSE and should include NARRATIVE or DESCRIPTIVE details to establish the main lines of the plot. Do not forget that lack of variety in plot and language skills is typical of Grade 3. Accuracy is the criterion to establish here.

Grade 4's **simple plot** will approach the adequacy of Grade 3 but may be poorly organised or have significant inaccuracies.

5 : 6 Grade 5's **very basic plot** will occasionally try to achieve particular effects, and it will also be poorly organised and have significant inaccuracies.

Grade 6 will have a combination of negative features, will be **rambling**, or have **obscurities** in the plot and the Marker will have difficulty in decoding because of very poor spelling, sentencing, or handwriting.

NB If candidates ignore the rubric in respect of plot or character this may place them in Grade 5 in terms of purpose ('few signs of appropriateness'), unless there are other strong compensating features ('accurate', 'varied', 'sensitive'). Where there are no strong compensating features, this may tip the balance overall into Grade 6.

Discursive/Informative Numbers 2, 5, 6, 10, 13, 17, 19.
Task specifications/rubrics/purposes
The rubrics cover controversial issues which are likely to elicit emotional responses. Objectivity is not required but clear, straightforward presentation of a point of view is required. At all levels, candidates must deal with the specific topics or, as is the case in one of the tasks, use the imposed format to convey information about a specific activity.

No 2 agree/disagree or balanced view. Candidates may choose to deal with the topic from one particular point of view or take a more balanced approach. Personal/anecdotal evidence may very well figure but should be used to support the candidate's line of argument.

No 5 imposed format of informative article for a magazine although the purpose here is W1 to convey information.

No 6 agree/disagree or balanced view. Personal/anecdotal evidence may feature but this should enhance the argument.

No 10 agree only. Additionally, candidates must adopt the imposed format of the magazine article although the purpose is persuasive/argumentative. It is also possible that candidates could present the case for more than one group of animals.

No 13 agree/disagree or balanced view. Personal/anecdotal evidence is very likely to be used but it should reinforce a line of argument.

No 17 agree/disagree or balanced. Again, personal/anecdotal evidence may well feature but this should be used to support the line of thought adopted by the candidate.

No 19 agree/disagree or balanced view. Personal/anecdotal evidence may feature but this should enhance the argument.

Grade Differentiation – Discursive

1 : 2 Grade 1 responses will show a **combination of depth, complexity and skilful deployment** of ideas, and will also marshall evidence in support of an argument. Grade 2 responses will lack this combination of technical skill and confident tone, presenting ideas in a **less developed** or **sustained** manner.

3 : 4 Grade 3 will attempt an orderly flow of ideas, which may not succeed logically, whereas Grade 4 will be typically **weak in structure**, or **have thin ideas** or poorly constructed sentences.

5 : 6 Grade 5 will present ideas and opinions in **concrete, personal terms** which may be anecdotal, but are more than a bald series of unsupported, **disjointed** or **rambling** statements, the hallmarks of Grade 6.

Grade Differentiation – Informative

1 : 2 Grade 1 will convey information in a **clear sequence, selecting and highlighting** what is most significant. Grade 2 responses will be **less well sustained** in terms of the qualities of distinction in **ideas, construction and language**.

3 : 4 Grade 3 will convey the relevant information **in some kind of sequence** which may not succeed logically, whereas Grade 4 will be **weak in structure** or have **thin ideas** or **weak sentence construction**.

5 : 6 Grade 5 will convey only **simple information**. Formal errors will be obtrusive but the writing will not be marked by the **rambling** and **disjointed** statements which define Grade 6.

Personal Experience/Descriptive Numbers: 1, 8, 9, 12, 15, 18, 20.
Task specifications/rubric/purposes
Each of the above calls for a personal response; while there are no genre requirements here, content must be specific and appropriate.

No 1 the rubric restricts the candidate to a single school trip to a city.

No 8 the rubric restricts the candidate to a single sporting occasion when taking part was more important than winning.

No 9 candidates should stress the importance of a pet in their lives, although reference made to more than one pet would still be acceptable.

No 12 candidates must write about a single occasion although they must also describe the struggle to achieve the personal goal. Some latitude should be given here with reference to the ideas of 'struggle' and 'personal'.

No 15   the rubric restricts candidates to a single occasion although this may be spread over time. Candidates should focus on the new skills gained from involvement in an outdoor activity.

No 18   description of a scene is an explicit requirement. Candidates should choose ONE of the options.

No 20   the rubric restricts the candidate to a single occasion although, again, this may be spread over time. Candidates should also focus on how they became positive role models for a friend or a relative.

Grade Differentiation

1 : 2   Grade 1 will be a well crafted, stylish account and will deploy a range of skills to express perceptiveness and self-awareness and to achieve or create effects, while a Grade 2 account will be soundly constructed and show a **measure of insight** and self-awareness expressed accurately. Grade 2 may not be succinct but will be **substantial**.

3 : 4   A Grade 3 response will be reasonably well sustained, with easily grasped structure, and will on the whole be correct but with a certain dull monotony.
Grade 4 will be structurally weak and thin in ideas but will still **attempt involvement, approaching the overall adequacy** of Grade 3.

5 : 6   Grade 5 may have positive features such as a runaway enthusiasm which may detract from the stated purpose but it will present the **gist** of the experience without **ramblings** and **incoherence** which, along with **numerous errors** and near-illegible handwriting are the mark of Grade 6.

Free Choice Numbers: 4.
Task specification/rubric/purposes
This question calls for the candidate to determine the purpose of the writing and format. It is, therefore, important that the candidate's writing purpose is made clear in the course of the response. Markers should assess according to the appropriate criteria.

No 4   the rubric restricts the candidate to the use of the picture and its associated ideas.

ENGLISH WRITING—2010

Narrative Numbers: 1, 7, 8, 13, 14, 20.
Task specifications/rubric/purposes
The criteria demand appropriate ideas and evidence of structure which in the narrative genre involve **plot** or **content** or **atmosphere**.

Note that the development of **setting** and **character** as well as **plot** is an explicit requirement for all of the short story options.

No 1   *short story* – imposed title, **The Rebel**, must be reflected in the narrative.

No 7   *short story* – imposed title, **The Smile**, must be reflected in the narrative.

No 8   *short story* – the imposed opening should be continued.

No 13   *short story* – the imposed opening should be continued.

No 14   *short story* – the imposed opening should be continued.

No 20   *short story* – imposed title, **The Arrival**, must be reflected in the narrative.

Grade Differentiation

1 : 2   Grade 1 narrative will show **overall distinction** in IDEAS, CONSTRUCTION and LANGUAGE, and will be both **stylish and skilful**, while Grade 2 narrative will fall short both in the quality and in the **combination** of skills.

3 : 4   Grade 3 responses will have an **appropriate plot**, will make use of appropriate **register** to create ATMOSPHERE or SUSPENSE and should include NARRATIVE or DESCRIPTIVE details to establish the main lines of the plot. Do not forget that lack of variety in plot and language skills is typical of Grade 3. Accuracy is the criterion to establish here.

Grade 4's **simple plot** will approach the adequacy of Grade 3 but may be poorly organised or have significant inaccuracies.

5 : 6   Grade 5's **very basic plot** will occasionally try to achieve particular effects, and it will also be poorly organised and have significant inaccuracies.

Grade 6 will have a combination of negative features, will be **rambling**, or have **obscurities** in the plot and the Marker will have difficulty in decoding because of very poor spelling, sentencing, or handwriting.

NB   If candidates ignore the rubric in respect of plot or character this may place them in Grade 5 in terms of purpose ('few signs of appropriateness'), unless there are other strong compensating features ('accurate', 'varied', 'sensitive'). Where there are no strong compensating features, this may tip the balance overall into Grade 6.

Discursive/Informative Numbers 2, 4, 5, 9, 12, 18, 21.
Task specifications/rubrics/purposes
The rubrics cover controversial issues which are likely to elicit emotional responses. Objectivity is not required but clear, straightforward presentation of a point of view is required. At all levels, candidates must deal with the specific topics or, as is the case in one of the tasks, use the imposed format to convey information about a specific activity.

No 2   *agree/disagree or balanced view*. Candidates may choose to deal with the topic from one particular point of view or take a more balanced approach. Personal/anecdotal evidence may figure but should be used to support the candidate's argument.

No 4   *agree/disagree or balanced view*. Personal or anecdotal may feature but should follow a line of thought.

No 5   *agree/disagree/balanced*. Personal/anecdotal evidence may be present but this should follow a line of thought.

No 9 *agree/disagree/balanced.* Personal/anecdotal evidence may be present but this should follow a line of thought.

No 12 imposed format of article for school magazine, although the purpose is clearly discursive. Candidates must present the case either for or against the notion of Scottish independence.

No 18 imposed format of school magazine article although the genre required straddles description and W1 information. Note that there is no requirement for candidates to include thoughts and feelings.

No 21 is a W1 informative piece on the life skills the candidate would like to learn at school. While three possibilities are listed, the candidate need not use any of these.

Grade Differentiation – Discursive

1 : 2 *Grade 1* responses will show a **combination of depth, complexity and skilful deployment** of ideas, and will also marshall evidence in support of an argument.
Grade 2 responses will lack this combination of technical skill and confident tone, presenting ideas in a **less developed** or **sustained** manner.

3 : 4 *Grade 3* will attempt an orderly flow of ideas, which may not succeed logically, whereas *Grade 4* will be typically **weak in structure**, or **have thin ideas** or poorly constructed sentences.

5 : 6 *Grade 5* will present ideas and opinions in **concrete, personal terms** which may be anecdotal, but are more than a bald series of unsupported, **disjointed** or **rambling** statements, the hallmarks of *Grade 6*.

Grade Differentiation – Informative

1 : 2 *Grade 1* will convey information in a **clear sequence, selecting and highlighting** what is most significant.
Grade 2 responses will be **less well sustained** in terms of the qualities of distinction in **ideas, construction and language**.

3 : 4 *Grade 3* will convey the relevant information **in some kind of sequence** which may not succeed logically, whereas *Grade 4* will be **weak in structure** or have **thin ideas** or **weak sentence construction**.

5 : 6 *Grade 5* will convey only **simple information**. Formal errors will be obtrusive but the writing will not be marked by the **rambling** and **disjointed** statements which define *Grade 6*.

Personal Experience/Descriptive Numbers: 3, 6, 10, 11, 15, 17, 19.

Task specifications/rubric/purposes

Each of the above calls for a personal response; while there are no genre requirements here, content must be specific and appropriate.

No 3 the single occasion may be used as a catalyst for a range of life-changing experiences.

No 6 candidates must write about a single occasion when breaking a rule was more important than following it.

No 10 the rubric restricts the candidates to a specific fairground attraction. Description of the place must feature. Thoughts and feelings should also be included.

No 11 candidates must write about a single occasion and some latitude may be required on the idea of a Scottish celebration or festival. Equally, candidates may choose to write about their involvement in a number of different aspects of the celebration or festival.

No 15 the rubric restricts to a single occasion although this may be spread over time. The way in which the candidate felt second best should be made clear.

No 17 the description of a scene is required from ONE of two choices.

No 19 candidates must write about a single occasion when they were given good advice but did not take it.

Grade Differentiation

1 : 2 *Grade 1* will be a well crafted, stylish account and will deploy a range of skills to express perceptiveness and self-awareness and to achieve or create effects, while a *Grade 2* account will be soundly constructed and show a **measure of insight** and self-awareness expressed accurately. *Grade 2* may not be succinct but will be substantial.

3 : 4 A *Grade 3* response will be reasonably well sustained, with easily grasped structure, and will on the whole be correct but with a certain dull monotony.
Grade 4 will be structurally weak and thin in ideas but will still **attempt involvement, approaching the overall adequacy** of *Grade 3*.

5 : 6 *Grade 5* may have positive features such as a runaway enthusiasm which may detract from the stated purpose but it will present the *gist* of the experience without **ramblings** and **incoherence** which, along with **numerous errors** and near-illegible handwriting are the mark of *Grade 6*.

Free Choice Number: 16.

Task specification/rubric/purposes

This question calls for the candidate to determine the purpose of the writing and format. It is, therefore, important that the candidate's writing purpose is made clear in the course of the response. Markers should assess according to the appropriate criteria.

No 16 the rubric restricts the candidate to the use of the picture and its associated ideas.

ENGLISH WRITING—2011

Narrative Numbers: 1, 4, 9, 11, 15, 20.
Task specifications/rubric/purposes
The criteria demand appropriate ideas and evidence which in the narrative genre involve **plot** or **content** or **atmosphere**.
Note that the development of **setting** and **character** as well as **plot** is an explicit requirement for all of the short story options.

No 1   *short story* – imposed opening should be continued.
No 4   *short story* – choice of imposed titles from which the candidates must select ONE from either **Overboard** or **The Boat.** The title selected must be reflected in the narrative.
No 9   *short story* – choice of imposed titles from which the candidates must select ONE from either **The Experiment** or **The Monster**. The title selected must be reflected in the narrative.
No 11 *short story* – imposed opening should be continued.
No 15 *short story* – imposed title **Sunset** must be reflected in the narrative.
No 20 *short story* – imposed title **Escape from the City** must be reflected in the narrative.

Grade Differentiation
1 : 2   *Grade 1* narrative will show **overall distinction** in IDEAS, CONSTRUCTION and LANGUAGE, and will be both **stylish and skilful**, while *Grade 2* narrative will fall short both in the quality and in the **combination** of skills.
3 : 4   *Grade 3* responses will have an **appropriate plot**, will make use of appropriate **register** to create ATMOSPHERE or SUSPENSE and should include NARRATIVE or DESCRIPTIVE details to establish the main lines of the plot. Do not forget that lack of variety in plot and language skills is typical of *Grade 3*. Accuracy is the criterion to establish here.
           Grade 4's **simple plot** will approach the adequacy of *Grade 3* but may be poorly organised or have significant inaccuracies.
5 : 6   *Grade 5*'s **very basic plot** will occasionally try to achieve particular effects, and it will also be poorly organised and have significant inaccuracies.
           Grade 6 will have a combination of negative features, will be **rambling**, or have **obscurities** in the plot and the Marker will have difficulty in decoding because of very poor spelling, sentencing, or handwriting.
NB   If candidates ignore the rubric in respect of plot or character this may place them in *Grade 5* in terms of purpose ('few signs of appropriateness'), unless there are other strong compensating features ('accurate', 'varied', 'sensitive'). Where there are no strong compensating features, this may tip the balance overall into *Grade 6*.

Discursive/Informative Numbers: 3, 5, 8, 12, 19.
Task specifications/rubrics/purposes
The rubrics cover controversial topics which are likely to elicit emotional responses. Objectivity is not required but clear, straightforward presentation of a point of view is required. At all levels, candidates must deal with the specific topics.

No 3   *agree/disagree or balanced view*. Candidates may choose to deal with the topic from one particular point of view or take a more balanced approach. Personal/anecdotal evidence may well feature but this should be used to progress a line of thought.
No 5   *agree/disagree or balanced view*. Personal/anecdotal evidence may well feature but this should be used to progress a line of thought. Some latitude may be required in the interpretation of the idea of risk.
No 8   *agree/disagree or balanced view*. Personal/anecdotal evidence may well feature but this should be used to reinforce the argument.
No 12 *agree/disagree or balanced view*. Personal/anecdotal evidence may very well feature but, again this should be used to pursue a line of thought.
No 19 *agree/disagree or balanced view*. Personal/anecdotal evidence may very well feature but, again, this should be used to pursue a line of thought. Some latitude may be required in the interpretation of the idea of a city.

Grade Differentiation – Discursive
1 : 2   *Grade 1* responses will show a **combination of depth, complexity and skilful deployment** of ideas, and will also marshall evidence in support of an argument.
           Grade 2 responses will lack this combination of technical skill and confident tone, presenting ideas in a **less developed** or **sustained** manner.
3 : 4   *Grade 3* will attempt an orderly flow of ideas, which may not succeed logically, whereas *Grade 4* will be typically **weak in structure**, or **have thin ideas** or poorly constructed sentences.
5 : 6   *Grade 5* will present ideas and opinions in **concrete, personal terms** which may be anecdotal, but are more than a bald series of unsupported, **disjointed** or **rambling** statements, the hallmarks of *Grade 6*.

Grade Differentiation – Informative
1 : 2   *Grade 1* will convey information in a **clear sequence, selecting and highlighting** what is most significant. *Grade 2* responses will be **less well sustained** in terms of the qualities of distinction in **ideas, construction and language.**
3 : 4   *Grade 3* will convey the relevant information **in some kind of sequence** which may not succeed logically, whereas *Grade 4* will be **weak in structure** or have **thin ideas** or **weak sentence construction**.
5 : 6   *Grade 5* will convey only **simple information**. Formal errors will be obtrusive but the writing will not be marked by the **rambling** and **disjointed** statements which define *Grade 6*.

Personal Experience/Descriptive Numbers: 2, 6, 10, 13, 14, 17, 18.

No 2   the rubric restricts the candidate to a single occasion when they receive a telephone call giving unwelcoming news.
No 6   candidates must write about a single occasion in which the memorable nature of the boat journey should be conveyed through their feelings and reactions.
No 10 the rubric restricts the candidate to one instance when science or technology had a life changing impact. It should be noted that the distinction between science or technology is not the significant factor here.
No 13 there is no restriction to a single occasion here. There is also the possibility here of some informative writing although candidates are reminded that thoughts and feelings should be rendered.
No 14 the rubric restricts candidates to a single occasion although this may be spread over time. Some latitude in the interpretation of the connotations of 'childhood' may be appropriate.
No 17 description of a scene is an explicit requirement. Candidates should choose ONE of the options.
No 18 description of a local park is an explicit requirement, although markers should exercise latitude over the interpretation of a 'local' park.

Grade Differentiation

1 : 2   *Grade 1* will be a well crafted, stylish account and will deploy a range of skills to express perceptiveness and self-awareness and to achieve or create effects, while a *Grade 2* account will be soundly constructed and show a **measure of insight** and self-awareness expressed accurately. *Grade 2* may not be succinct but will be substantial.

3 : 4   A *Grade 3* response will be reasonably well sustained, with easily grasped structure, and will on the whole be correct but with a certain dull monotony.
Grade 4 will be structurally weak and thin in ideas but will still **attempt involvement, approaching the overall adequacy** of *Grade 3*.

5 : 6   *Grade 5* may have positive features such as a runaway enthusiasm which may detract from the stated purpose but it will present the **gist** of the experience without **ramblings** and **incoherence** which, along with **numerous errors** and near-illegible handwriting are the mark of *Grade 6*.

Free Choice Number: 7, 16.

This question calls for the candidate to determine the purpose of the writing and format. It is, therefore, important that the candidate's writing purpose is made clear in the course of the response. Markers should assess according to the appropriate criteria.

No 7   the rubric restricts the candidate to the use of the picture and its associated ideas.

No 16   the rubric restricts the candidate to the use of the picture and its associated ideas.

ENGLISH WRITING—2012

Narrative Numbers: 3, 9, 12, 16, 23.
Task specifications/rubric/purposes

The criteria demand appropriate ideas and evidence which in the narrative genre involve **plot** or **content** or **atmosphere**.
Note that the development of **setting** and **character** as well as **plot** is an explicit requirement for all of the short story options.

No 3   *short story* – imposed title **The Treasure Hunt** must be reflected in the narrative.

No 9   *short story* – imposed opening should be continued.

No 12   *short story* – imposed opening should be continued.

No 16   *short story* – imposed title **No Fear** must be reflected in the narrative.

No 23   *short story* – imposed title **The High Life** must be reflected in the narrative.

Grade Differentiation

1 : 2   *Grade 1* narrative will show **overall distinction** in IDEAS, CONSTRUCTION and LANGUAGE, and will be both **stylish and skilful**, while *Grade 2* narrative will fall short both in the quality and in the **combination** of skills.

3 : 4   *Grade 3* responses will have an **appropriate plot**, will make use of appropriate **register** to create ATMOSPHERE or SUSPENSE and should include NARRATIVE or DESCRIPTIVE details to establish the main lines of the plot. Do not forget that lack of variety in plot and language skills is typical of *Grade 3*. Accuracy is the criterion to establish here.
Grade 4's **simple plot** will approach the adequacy of *Grade 3* but may be poorly organised or have significant inaccuracies.

5 : 6   *Grade 5*'s **very basic plot** will occasionally try to achieve particular effects, and it will also be poorly organised and have significant inaccuracies.
Grade 6 will have a combination of negative features, will be **rambling**, or have **obscurities** in the plot and the Marker will have difficulty in decoding because of very poor spelling, sentencing, or handwriting.

NB   If candidates ignore the rubric in respect of plot or character this may place them in *Grade 5* in terms of purpose ('few signs of appropriateness'), unless there are other strong compensating features ('accurate', 'varied', 'sensitive'). Where there are no strong compensating features, this may tip the balance overall into *Grade 6*.

Discursive/Informative Numbers: 1, 5, 7, 10, 13, 15, 18, 20, 22.
Task specifications/rubrics/purposes

The rubrics cover controversial topics which are likely to elicit emotional responses. Objectivity is not required but clear, straightforward presentation of a point of view is required. At all levels, candidates must deal with the specific topics.

No 1   *agree/disagree or balanced view*. Candidates may choose to deal with the topic from one particular point of view or take a more balanced approach. Personal/anecdotal evidence may well feature but this should be used to progress a line of thought.

No 5   *agree/disagree or balanced view*. Personal/anecdotal evidence may very well feature but this should be used to progress a line of thought. It is also possible (and entirely acceptable) that candidates may choose to write from a personal/reflective standpoint.

No 7   *candidates are required to convey information*/describe a visit to a place of historic interest (some latitude might be required in the interpretation of this) through the medium of an article.

No 10 *agree/disagree or balanced view.* Again, personal/anecdotal evidence may well feature but this should be used to reinforce the argument.

No 13 *agree/disagree or balanced view.* Personal/anecdotal evidence may very well feature but, again, this should be used to pursue a line of thought.

No 15 *candidates are required to convey information* about an interesting sport or pastime through the medium of an article. Some latitude might be required in the interpretation of 'interesting,' 'sport,' and 'pastime'.

No 18 *agree/disagree or balanced view.* Personal/anecdotal evidence may feature but, this should be used to pursue a line of thought.

No 20 *agree/disagree or balanced view.* Personal/anecdotal evidence may very well feature but, again this should be used to pursue a line of thought.

No 22 *agree/disagree or balanced view.* Personal/anecdotal evidence may very well feature but, again this should be used to pursue a line of thought.

Grade Differentiation – Discursive

1 : 2 *Grade 1* responses will show a **combination of depth, complexity and skilful deployment** of ideas, and will also marshall evidence in support of an argument.
Grade 2 responses will lack this combination of technical skill and confident tone, presenting ideas in a **less developed** or **sustained** manner.

3 : 4 *Grade 3* will attempt an orderly flow of ideas, which may not succeed logically, whereas *Grade 4* will be typically **weak in structure**, or **have thin ideas** or poorly constructed sentences.

5 : 6 *Grade 5* will present ideas and opinions in **concrete, personal terms** which may be anecdotal, but are more than a bald series of unsupported, **disjointed** or **rambling** statements, the hallmarks of *Grade 6*.

Grade Differentiation – Informative

1 : 2 *Grade 1* will convey information in a **clear sequence**, **selecting and highlighting** what is most significant.
Grade 2 responses will be **less well sustained** in terms of the qualities of distinction in **ideas, construction and language**.

3 : 4 *Grade 3* will convey the relevant information **in some kind of sequence** which may not succeed logically, whereas *Grade 4* will be **weak in structure** or have **thin ideas** or **weak sentence construction**.

5 : 6 *Grade 5* will convey only **simple information**. Formal errors will be obtrusive but the writing will not be marked by the **rambling** and **disjointed** statements which define *Grade 6*.

Personal Experience/Descriptive Numbers: 2, 4, 6, 8, 11, 17, 19, 21.

No 2 the rubric restricts the candidate to a single occasion when they felt compelled to buy something new. It is possible that there will be an element of the discursive evident if candidates elect to justify or rationalise the process.

No 4 description of the scene suggested by the picture is an explicit requirement.

No 6 the rubric restricts the candidate to one instance when they made a fresh start. In the interpretation of 'fresh start,' some latitude might be required.

No 8 the rubric restricts the candidate to the importance of **musical** performance to them. Note that this rubric will allow for several performances to be addressed.

No 11 the rubric restricts candidates to a single occasion when their school was closed because of the weather. The ensuing events might be spread over time. Note that the idea of unexpected fun is merely a suggestion; it is not absolutely necessary.

No 17 the rubric restricts the candidate to a single occasion when the preparation for a competition was as important as the competition itself. Both sides of the rubric must be addressed.

No 19 description of **ONE** of the two scenes is an explicit requirement.

No 21 the rubric restricts the candidate to the one place in the world they would really like to visit, although it should be noted that this task could cross over into the discursive-giving reasons for the choice.

Grade Differentiation

1 : 2 *Grade 1* will be a well crafted, stylish account and will deploy a range of skills to express perceptiveness and self-awareness and to achieve or create effects, while a *Grade 2* account will be soundly constructed and show a **measure of insight** and self-awareness expressed accurately. *Grade 2* may not be succinct but will be substantial.

3 : 4 A *Grade 3* response will be reasonably well sustained, with easily grasped structure, and will on the whole be correct but with a certain dull monotony.
Grade 4 will be structurally weak and thin in ideas but will still **attempt involvement, approaching the overall adequacy** of *Grade 3*.

5 : 6 *Grade 5* may have positive features such as a runaway enthusiasm which may detract from the stated purpose but it will present the **gist** of the experience without **ramblings** and **incoherence** which, along with **numerous errors** and near-illegible handwriting are the mark of *Grade 6*.

Free Choice Number: 14.

This question calls for the candidate to determine the purpose of the writing and format. It is, therefore, important that the candidate's writing purpose is made clear in the course of the response. Markers should assess according to the appropriate criteria.

No 14 the rubric restricts the candidate to the use of the picture and its associated ideas.

Hey! I've done it